THE LINE OF FAITH

Brian

Heb 11:6

THE LINE OF FAITH

40 DAYS TO DEEPER DEPENDENCY

Bill Elliff

Graceful Truth Series

THE LINE OF FAITH
40 Days to Deeper Dependency
By Bill Elliff

Published by TruthInk Publications
6600 Crystal Hill Road
North Little Rock, Arkansas 72118

© 2016 by Bill Elliff

Cover Design: Keith Runkle

ISBN 9780983116820
ISBN: 0983116822

Printed in the United Sates of America

*Dedicated to Manley Beasley, E.F. "Preacher" Hallock,
and my father, J.T. Elliff*

Three heroes who taught this young learner about faith.

LEARNING FROM

THE FATHER OF OUR FAITH

D A Y   1

THE LINE OF FAITH

"Then he believed in the Lord and
He reckoned it to him as righteousness."

GENESIS 15:6

EVERYTHING IN YOUR life is about faith. Everything. The trajectory of your life is determined by the depth of your dependency on God.

If you genuinely believe right now that God is sovereign and good and knows what He's doing, you are not upset with the difficulties of life. If you believe that He is a Provider who knows your needs before you ask Him and will freely give you all things, you are not gripped with fear at what looks like lack or poor timing on God's part. If you are confident that He is the Savior and you have trusted in Him for your salvation, the prospect of eternity does not frighten, but delights you. If you embrace the truth that God is the owner of all, you do not balk when He directs you regarding the possessions over which He has made you a steward.

FATHER ABRAHAM

God came to Abram promising he would give him children, as many as the "stars of the sky." Abram had a choice: to believe what his body and the circumstances told him or to count God's character as true. We are forever grateful for his choice.

"Then he believed," the Bible records. The moment the line of faith was crossed, counting God true, God counted Abram as one who believed. He was right in his faith before God. And the results proved the faithfulness of God and His promises.

YOUR LINE

God is looking for people who will trust Him. Those who choose not to believe miss the best that God offers. The unbelieving are separated from Him and His work. Jesus left His own hometown saying He could do nothing there because of their unbelief.

You may not realize it, but how you handle your finances, forgive those who've hurt you, embrace trials, accept hardship, deal with your sin, is all taking you to the line. Will you cross over? Will you believe in the character of God who is the Provider, Forgiver, Sustainer, Savior?

YOUR LOSS AND GOD'S

The great tragedy of our unbelief is that we lose that for which we were created. We were designed to walk in the garden with God. The only path to this is dependence upon our Creator. Our First Parents lost the sweetness of fellowship, the provision of the Father, the direction of the ultimate Leader and more. And when we follow in their footsteps the loss continues.

And God misses something also. He made us for Himself. Our unbelief is a slap in His face and a rejection of His plan. Someone who questions your character, doubts your motives, or distrusts your purposes gives you the greatest relational backhand. To say they believe you and then act differently behind your back is the worst kind of betrayal.

For us, spiritual unbelief is a whim—a light thing that can be easily tossed about. Not so with God. Unbelief grieves the Creator's heart, for He has so much planned. Prideful unbelief is the root of every sin that has infected His creation.

Over the coming years God will confront you with thousands of chances to get in on His agenda. He will bring you to the line.

Where is the line of faith in your life right now? You are always there. God is challenging you to believe in Him. The great question is always, "What do you really believe about God and what are you believing Him for *right now?*

D A Y 2

Simple Moment | PROFOUND FAITH

THE BIBLE IS full of stories of ordinary men and women who were confronted in ordinary moments by our extraordinary God. At each point they were always faced with the same choice: *"Will I believe what God says or not?" "Will I act like what God says is true?" "Will I adjust my life to make room for the possibility that God is about to do what He says in and through me?"*

Those who believed are the ones we now embrace as the great heroes of the faith, (see Hebrews, Chapter 11, for a partial listing of these men and women). I doubt they saw themselves this way. They probably never realized the magnitude of the moment or the significance of their choice in the story of God's interaction with humanity. Nor do we.

ABRAM'S MOMENT

Abram had refused to accept a reward from the King of Sodom, as seen in Genesis 14. In the next moment, recorded in Genesis 15, God comes in a vision and promises Abram a *greater* reward. Abram says, "Lord, the one thing I want is a child (which You promised earlier). Why am I childless?" That was the reward he wanted. It is an honest cry from a concerned, confused heart.

In answer to this honesty, God gives Abram a further confirmation of His earlier promise. Pointing to the stars, he tells him that his descendants will be as the stars of the heaven. He gave his servant a word from above. God opened up His kingdom and showed Abram what was already there. Abram was then faced with the choice to believe or mistrust what He had seen. His decision would be used to help God's "kingdom come and will be done on earth as it is in heaven," in ways beyond his imagining.

"And he believed the Lord, and He counted it to him as righteousness" (Genesis 15:6). This verse is referenced four times in the New Testament, (Romans 4:3, 22; Galatians 3:6; James 2:23), and is used as one of the great illustrations of faith.

You wonder if Abram had any idea that this interchange would be so historic and instructive for millions. That those who wrestled with faith in every century to follow would be encouraged and educated by his honest cry, God's clear promise, and Abram's childlike response of faith. That this exchange was a profound moment of redemptive destiny.

YOUR MOMENT

Is God any different? If not, it would seem that God desires to do the same today. That He responds to our confusion and concern. That He still speaks. That He challenges us to take Him at His word. That He can give grace for us to believe. That He is still creating redemptive movements and, in the process, making faith-heroes through His word and man's faith. And that He "counts" our faith unto righteousness.

Your experience under the stars may be waiting for you today. It may even come at a time of great confusion and concern. Look for it. Don't miss the chance to encounter God and be used of Him to affect millions who follow. He is calling you—in your simple moment—to profound faith.

DAY 3

THE PROGRESSION OF YOUR FAITH

Without becoming weak in faith he contemplated
his own body, now as good as dead since he was
about a hundred years old, and the deadness of
Sarah's womb; yet, with respect to the promise of
God, he did not waver in unbelief but grew strong
in faith, giving glory to God, and being fully as-
sured that what God had promised, He was able
also to perform. Therefore it was also credited to
him as righteousness.

ROMANS 4:19-22

THE GREAT POINT of Romans, Chapter Four, is to show the
Jews, (and all thereafter), that even their greatest ancestor,
Abraham, was made acceptable to God through faith, not
through his own works.

In the midst of this chapter, Paul gives us several clear
explanations of faith's composition. Genuine belief is always
the same. It may come in different degrees and be forged
on different anvils, but authentic trust always runs down the
same path.

THE PROMISE
" yet with respect to the promise of God " (Vs. 20)

Abraham had been given a promise from God that he would have a son who would be the beginning of an entire race. The challenge of faith was, "Will I believe what God has said?" Paul would later say "faith comes by hearing and hearing by the word of God." This is where it always begins.

You may think that there is no promise about your current situation or need, so you are not called upon to believe. But that is not true. There are 7,000 promises in God's word (an average of *seven* promises on every page of your Bible!) This is one of God's primary operating systems with you. It is your responsibility to be listening to Him through the Word daily and asking, "What does God say to me and call me to believe about my day? My current situation? The issues that surround me?" If you are listening with a willing heart He will speak.

THE CONTEMPLATION
"Without becoming weak in faith he contemplated his own body, now as good as dead since he was about a hundred years old, and the deadness of Sarah's womb" (Vs. 19)

Once seeing what God has said about your issue, it is natural to consider the magnitude of God's statements in relation to the problem. Abraham was 99 years old. His wife was 89. He considered this. He pondered, thought about, wondered, whether God would be able to do what He promised. This is a natural progression in faith.

For instance, you may have a financial need. There is no seeming possibility for it to be met, but then you read the promise God spoke through Paul: "My God will supply all of your needs according to His riches in glory in Christ Jesus" (Philippians 4:19). Now, you have a dilemma and you consider this. In light of your current reality, is there a *greater* reality? Something bigger than what your eyes can see? Is what God said true for me in this issue?

THE UNWAVERING BELIEF
"With respect to the promise of God, he did not waver in unbelief"
(Vs. 20)

Abraham chose to take God at His Word. Despite the apparent obstacles and contradictions to his logical reasoning, he believed God would do what He said. At this moment, Abraham chose to embrace God's greater reality. He crossed the line of faith.

Faith is most powerful when it is against all odds. When it believes in a God who "calls into existence things that do not exist." In fact, that is the real definition of faith. It is believing something we cannot see based upon the faithfulness of the One who sees all.

God has created a system that *makes us* trust Him. The only way we can function properly in this world (or the next) is through faith. And to insure this posture, God is constantly asking us to hope against hope, to believe in the impossible, to trust that He can and will do what is not seen and is contrary to human reasoning.

THE STRENGTHENING
"but grew strong in faith" (Vs. 20)

Abraham's honest contemplation and continued belief strengthened His faith. F.F. Bruce said, "Having nothing to rest upon but the bare word of God, he relied on that, in face of all the opposing indications which pressed on him from every side. In fact, his faith was strengthened by the very force of the obstacles which lay in its path."

THE THANKSGIVING
" giving glory to God" (Vs. 20)

The apex of faith is the gratitude that gives thanks even before we see the promise fulfilled, even in spite of obstacles. This is the confidence that says, "I believe God! He will not fail me! He has said 'My God shall supply all your needs' and I know that He will honor His Word."

THE FULL ASSURANCE
" being fully assured that what God had promised, He was able also to perform." (Vs. 21)

Abraham came to the point where he was not doubting or wavering. This was the completing of his faith. A confidence that would not be shaken and would cross the finish line of faith.

THE CREDIT
"Therefore it was also credited to him as righteousness." (Vs. 22)

Such faith means something to God. It honors Him and God says that Abraham's faith was "credited to him as righteousness." His faith is what put Abraham in right standing with a holy God. Anything less would have been unacceptable.

The reason for this is simple: "For this reason it is by faith, in order that it may be in accordance with grace," Paul says, (Romans 4:16). In God's plan, all the blessings, answers, provisions, and results that come from a faith exchange are an act of God's grace. We cannot claim any credit for their arrival.

Our part has been simply to believe with our head and heart in complete alignment, with our body in instant obedience, (even Abraham's continued physical relations with his wife was an act of faith), and with our mouth in continued confession that God is going to be faithful to His promises.

With every fiber of our being, every single day, we are to walk and talk as if what God says is completely true.

And, when God fulfills His promises, (and He always fulfills His promises because He cannot deny Himself), there are multitudes who are blessed, but only One who is glorified.

TESTING

"After these things, God tested Abraham."

(GENESIS 22:1)

GOD IS RUTHLESSLY interested in your faith. He will use everything at His disposal to develop you into a person who trusts Him. He knows that your life, the life and salvation of those around you, and His glory are all at stake. He knows that you will miss everything essential if you become a person who will not trust Him—a trust manifested by instant obedience to His leadership.

GOD'S BEST TOOL

One of God's best instruments in His Faith-Development-Tool-Bag is testing. Many people recoil at this idea. "How could a loving God do such a thing? It's not possible that He would allow or cause circumstances to come upon us just to test us," they reason.

Really? If you knew that your son or daughter could only be developed by tests and that those tests were absolutely essential to their best interest, would you use the same method? If you wouldn't, you might actually be harming them—unwilling to make the hard choices that would prepare them for a life that will call for the character only testing produces.

ABRAHAM'S EXAM

God tested Abraham. And this test was one of the most excruciating ever recorded in human history.

"**Abraham,**" God said as He called him by name.

"**Here am I,**" was Abraham's faithful response. "I am here, I am waiting, I am ready for the next step in the unfolding journey of faith you have for me."

"**Take your son**" This was the one possession he had that was uniquely his. Isaac had come from Abraham's very body. If ever there was something that Abraham could have clung to saying, "No, this is mine. I have the sole rights to this," it was Isaac. God tested him at the level of his dearest possession.

"**your only son**" Not only was it his most precious possession, but it was the only son Abraham had. He did not have multiple sons with Sarah. Only Isaac. This was compounded by the fact that Abraham knew the unique place that Isaac held as the lynch pin to all the promises of God. The covenant God had made hinged on the life and health of this boy. Yet it was here—with this *only* son—that God threw his test at Abraham.

"**the son whom you love**" Abraham's passion for his child, which God understood, made this the ultimate test. There are things that we have that we do not love. To surrender them to God is no test at all. But the things we cherish and adore and value—for God to put His hand to these calls to us at the deepest level of trust. And there was nothing Abraham loved more than his son.

"and offer him as a burnt offering on the mountain I will tell you." We read this phrase with little emotion because we've heard it routinely. But imagine this moment. Strip off your familiarity with this account and it will take your breath away. Place Abraham's robe upon yourself and hear God calling you to take *your* son, your *only* son, the son whom you *love* and place him on an altar, cutting his throat and burning him as a sacrifice.

Before you react in horror towards God, add one more log to the fire of your concerns. The Bible, written inerrantly by God Himself, describes this as a "test." It was a specific action, orchestrated directly by God, to see the extent of Abraham's faith and develop him into a man of uncompromising confidence in his Father.

THE PRODUCTION OF FAITH

The Apostle James would later explain to us why this method of God's is so essential.

> *"Count it all joy, my brethren, when you encounter various trials, knowing that the **testing** of your faith produces endurance* (i.e., faith stretched out, faith that will stand

fast). *But let that test have its complete result* (i.e., run its full course, do everything it was designed to do in you) *so that you will be perfect and complete."*

*"Blessed is the man who remains steadfast under trials, for after he has passed the **test** he will receive the crown of life"* (James 1:1-2, 12, *additions and emphasis mine*).

Why did Abraham not get upset at God for originating such an excruciating test, and how can we avoid such frustration ourselves?

Abraham was humble. "Here am I," he says twice in this passage. Abraham knew that God was the Creator with the absolute right to do anything He desired with that which He had made. This large and proper view of God kept him from the pride that makes a man think he's imposed upon when God takes him through difficult waters.

And Abraham knew something. He was no novice. He had been through this drill more than once and every time he cooperated with God he discovered that the tests were completely purposeful. With each exam the circumference of Abraham's faith expanded, preparing him for increasing faith in his journey to rightness and usefulness. God would always prove faithful and provide what was necessary. In short, Abraham knew God could be trusted. And so we see no resistance.

"So Abraham rose early in the morning, saddled his donkey and took two of his young men with him, and his

son Isaac." The depth of Abraham's confidence in God is indicated by the lack of questions. We have no record of Abraham's thoughts, fears, concerns. But what we do see is his immediate obedience. History records his faith, emphasized by rising up "early" to obey his Father.

THE ULTIMATE REWARDS

If you doubt the value of such an extraordinary and seemingly inhumane test, then look at the results. God was perfectly faithful—providing at the exact moment precisely what was needed—and Abraham was proven faithful. History will forever carry an amazing testimony of man's faith and God's faithfulness. Abraham will always be to us the measure of what faith is all about, encouraging us to believe God in the darkest trials and most challenging tests.

Abraham's exam was a test worth taking. And so is yours.

GOD'S FINAL EXAM

"After these things God tested Abraham."

(GENESIS 22:1)

GOD IS THE original trainer. He is in the business of developing men and women who can pass the most important tests and are prepared for every life challenge. In one of the seminal passages of scripture we learn some of the ways God tests Abraham.

This was at the close of Abraham's long life of faith and was his greatest test. This final exam embodied everything that Abraham had learned about trusting God.

THE LISTENING TEST
(God) said to him, "Abraham!" and he said, "Here am I." (Vs. 1)

The first test is "Are you listening? When I speak, will you hear Me and respond with rapt attention?"

THE TIMING TEST
"So Abraham rose early in the morning, saddled his donkey" (Vs. 3)

Obedience is doing what I'm told to do, WHEN I'M TOLD TO DO IT. To seek to obey two weeks later is not obedience at all. God is trying to develop men and women who will instantly respond to the prompting of His Spirit and the illumination of His Word.

THE MAN-FEARING TEST
Then Abraham said to his young men, "Stay here with the donkey; I and the boy will go over there and worship and come again to you." (Vs. 5)

We must be willing to stand in faith before others, not fearing at all what they will think. How many steps of faith have been aborted out of our fear of man? We must grow beyond this limiting, self-centered concern.

THE PROVISION TEST
Isaac said, …"Behold, the fire and the wood, but where is the lamb?" (Vs. 7)

Abraham said, "God will provide for himself the lamb for a burnt offering, my son." God is seeking to build men and women who will believe Him for every need of life.

Whether this was a veiled reference to Isaac that he was to be the sacrifice or rather that Abraham believed that God would provide another lamb, it was genuine confidence that God would give exactly what was needed when the time came.

THE SACRIFICE TEST

Abraham built the altar there and laid the wood in order and bound Isaac his son and laid him on the altar (Vs. 9)

The depth of a man's relationship and faith in the Father is always measured by this one question: "Will you sacrifice anything and everything, when called upon, for Me?" Abraham was asked for the ultimate surrender—his only son—the son of promise that he had waited for 100 years. And Abraham passed the test beautifully.

THE FLEXIBILITY TEST

But the angel of the Lord called to him from heaven …"Do not lay your hand on the boy." (Vs. 11)

Sometimes God tells us something for express purposes and then completely reverses directions. We realize in retrospect that the issue was not the issue—that God had another agenda all along.

Are we willing to turn 180 degrees at the slightest command of God?

THE FEAR TEST

"For now I know that you fear God, seeing you have not withheld your son, your only son, from me." (Vs. 12)

Do I fear God more than anyone or anything? Am I more interested in hearing the applause of heaven or earth? Am I willing to look foolish in the eyes of men to look wise in the eyes of God? Is God and His will my ultimate concern?

THE PERSEVERANCE TEST

Abraham stretched out his hand and took the knife to slay his son ... And Abraham lifted up his eyes and looked, and behold, behind him was a ram, caught in a thicket" (Vs. 10-13)

God had made a promise regarding Abraham's son. But at each juncture, God waited until the midnight hour to provide. God is in the habit of stretching his tests out to extract the full value.

Scripture indicates that Abraham may have believed God was going to resurrect Isaac after he sacrificed him. Abraham truly believed, as he expressed to his men, that he and the boy would worship and then return together. He believed in God and God's ultimate fulfillment of what was promised and he *kept believing* all the way to the end.

CHECK YOUR FAITH

Take a moment and evaluate your faith deeply, prayerfully, fully. How are you doing RIGHT NOW in the tests of faith?

God's Tests					My Current Score
1. Listening Test?	A	B	C	D	F
2. Timing Test?	A	B	C	D	F
3. Man-fearing Test?	A	B	C	D	F
4. Provision Test?	A	B	C	D	F
5. Sacrifice Test?	A	B	C	D	F
6. Flexibility Test?	A	B	C	D	F
7. Fear of God Test?	A	B	C	D	F
8. Perseverance Test?	A	B	C	D	F

THE JOY OF THE TEST

I once had a seminary teacher who would give us a single question on our exams for which we were to write a one-hour response. It was grueling, but he said, "I want this to be the most satisfying test you've ever taken." He knew that if we studied well and cooperated fully we would pass the test. The purpose of the test was not to hurt us, but to develop us. If we were ready, the testing actually brought great joy.

God's purpose in every test is to develop us and use us in ways beyond our imagination. Abraham had no idea that his simple acts on a solitary day would challenge and inspire believers for centuries. It may be hard for you to believe that God could forge a similar witness that would last for centuries through your faith. But He can.

LEARNING FROM

THE AUTHOR & FINISHER OF OUR FAITH

MAKING ROOM FOR GOD

IN GOD'S ECONOMY there is only one response we can make that pleases Him and opens the way for Him to be displayed as He desires in our daily lives. Over and over again Jesus' words in the Gospels record this fact. Notice the multiple times it's mentioned in just one chapter in Matthew's account.

> *And when Jesus saw their **faith**, he said to the paralytic, "Take heart, my son; your sins are forgiven." (Matthew 9:2)*

> *Jesus turned, and seeing her he said, "Take heart, daughter; your **faith** has made you well." And instantly the woman was made well. (Matthew 9:22)*

> *When he entered the house, the blind men came to him, and Jesus said to them, "Do you **believe** that I am able to do this?" They said to him, "Yes, Lord." (Matthew 9:28)*

Why did God record these rapid-fire, multiple accounts that all center on faith? He was not only raising the sick, but raising disciples. He was training the twelve and all of us who would read these accounts. His desire is to continually increase our faith capacity.

FAITH MAKES ROOM FOR GOD

Our unbelief aborts God's activity. Obviously, God can do whatever He desires, but when it comes to men and women, He has ordained that there must be one response to Him—to believe. And such faith opens the door for God to do what only God can do in and through us in every act of the common day.

This is consistent with Hebrews 11:6 which reminds us that, "Without faith it is impossible to please God." John would later add, "This is the victory that overcomes the world—our faith" (1 John 5:4).

FAITH BRINGS REWARD

It is stunning, particularly in light of what we deserve from God, that He chooses the word "reward" to indicate what He will do for those who trust Him. This is the same word He uses in Matthew, Chapter 6, when He reminds us to go in secret to pray and believe, and that He will reward this kind of faith openly. Faith is not only essential and encouraged, it is rewarded.

One of my mentors, Manley Beasley, would always ask me when he saw me, "Bill, what are you believing God for right now?" The first few times I was taken off-guard, but I soon learned that his was a legitimate question and a needed one. Those of us who are called to lead others must be first to cross the line into faith. Our faith must make room for God to be seen in the sphere of our leadership and ministry.

What a tragedy to go a week, a month, a year, a lifetime never illustrating to others that there is a God who works wonders.

Are you leading others to trust God for big things right now? Things that He has ordained which require the risk of faith? Things that will prove His ability to a watching world? Things that will show the world God's faithfulness?

Are you making room for God?

MISSING THE OBVIOUS

*The Pharisees and Sadducees came up, and testing
Jesus,
they asked Him to show them a sign from heaven.
But He replied to them …
"Do you know how to discern the appearance of the
sky, but cannot discern the signs of the times?" And
He left them and went away.*

(MATTHEW 16:1-4)

BLINDNESS IS COMPREHENSIVE. It allows a person to stand
in the presence of the obvious and be totally unaware.
Spiritual blindness, though, is a far greater disability.
Those with this disease can be blissfully oblivious and
eternally debilitated.

And, spiritual sight is essential for the exercise of faith.
If we do not see clearly what He is doing and instructing, we
will not know how to cooperate with Him in faith.

Once a group of so-called religious leaders stood in the
presence of the Son of God and did not recognize Him. The
depth of their spiritual darkness is seen in the silliness of

their request. They asked to see a sign from heaven while staring into the face of the single greatest Sign ever given!

NO SPIRITUAL RETINA

This can be explained in light of their lost condition. They did not have the Spirit of God. They could not see. But those of us who know Christ have no such excuse.

We have the ability to see. We hold multiple copies of God's clear revelation before us. Within us dwells the Interpreter of all truth who gives us the mind of Christ. Of all people, we should discern the signs of the times.

What is occurring before our eyes? When the economy bottoms out, is this merely a product of human failure or is there a Divine Voice shouting to materialistic people to repent? When terrorists crash into the World Trade Center on 9/11, does God have a word to say to the church? Is this manifestation of pure, unadulterated evil communicating anything to us about the state of our world in its rebellion to-ward God? Does the meteoric rise of a religion diametrically opposed to Christ and committed to the total annihilation of Christianity mean anything? When the worst immorality mentionable becomes our entertainment, can we not hear the deafening silence of God's removed hand (which is the worst kind of judgment)?

When "wars and rumors of wars" abound is there no bib-lical prophecy that puts this in context? If we looked back in history and observed a nation that killed one million babies a year for the sake of personal convenience, would we not see it for what it is?

TODAY'S SIGHTLESSNESS

Closer to home: when I lose my job, is God speaking? When my finances fail, is the Lord silent? As my marriage slowly crumbles, why do I not pick up on the signs of coming disaster and make necessary spiritual adjustments BEFORE the crisis occurs?

When the children of the church are turning away from Christ in record numbers as they reach adulthood, is this not shouting to us? When the church in America consistently fails to reproduce itself, shouldn't men and women recognize this decline and respond in repentance and revolutionary change led by God? Are we driving right past God's massive, neon billboards and never looking up?

If you find yourself with spiritual macular degeneration, cry out to God for healing. "Open my eyes, O Lord, that I may behold wonderful things from Thy law," the Psalmist prayed (Psalm 119:18).

The most sobering statement in this scenario with the Pharisees is the last: "And He left them and went away." Continued inattention to Christ can mean the loss of Christ. He moves on to those with eyes to see.

DAY 8

DOES HE FIND FAITH IN YOU?

*"When the Son of Man comes, will He find faith
on the earth?"*

(LUKE 18:7-8)

THAT PART OF us which is made in God's image hates injustice. When we are wrongly accused, our motives are questioned, or our rights trampled, we are often hurt and then angry. When we see a child abused, a clear criminal getting away, a dishonest leader prospering, something rises up within us. When we are cheated, lied to, or the recipient of hypocrisy, it registers. It is the cry for justice. Injustice hurts, and this world is filled with it and will be until the end.

THE ESSENTIAL CONNECTION
How do you respond when you experience injustice? It is ultimately determined by what you believe about God.

If you are not aware of God you will retaliate. It's the default mode of the unbelieving. The knee-jerk of the hurting is to hurt others—to seek revenge. It may be visible or underground. Fear may cause you to hold back your hand and not strike. But do not think this is not a response. Hurt builds like a river behind the dam of passivity. It may take time, but hurt will always push through. It will first seep, then flood. The one thing unresolved hurt will not do is remain static.

If you know God, your response should be driven by belief. As you are hurt, the questions are not, "Why did they hurt me?" or, "How can I seek revenge?" but, "Will I believe in God right now?" and, "What will I believe about Him?"

> " Now shall not God bring about justice for His elect, who cry to Him day and night, and will He delay long over them? I tell you that He will bring about justice for them speedily. However, when the Son of Man comes, will He find faith on the earth?" (Luke 18:7-8)

The believing know that God is the arbitrator of all injustice. He is the Judge and has promised to resolve inequity. We may not see it in this life, but it will be done.

THE PEACE THAT FAITH BRINGS

For those who know God intimately and believe in Him fully, a calm assurance awaits them. Initial pain can give way to peace like the sun shining through after a storm. If they remember that God is the Judge and Justifier of those who trust in Him they can trust the sovereignty of His authority and the perfection of His timing. The sting of injustice can push them to the One who is always just and always victorious.

Only the believing can rest retaliation in His faithful hands. Though some may mislabel this as passivity, it is an active response to the character of God. Once believing, there is no need for personal revenge.

> *"Never take your own revenge, beloved, but leave room for the wrath of God, for it is written, 'Vengeance is Mine, I will repay,' says the Lord." (Romans 12:17-19)*

The true believer waits on God's response and transfers the case to the Divine docket. When tempted to forget, they reassure their hearts through the promises of His Word and endure. Justice will be done and those who respond rightly will be rewarded.

> *"Therefore, do not throw away your confidence, which has a great reward.*
> *For you have need of endurance, so that when you have done the will of God, you may receive what was promised ... For yet in a very little while, He who is coming will come, and will not delay ... But My righteous one shall live by faith." (Hebrews 10:35-38)*

FAITH WAITS FOR THE FINAL SCENE

Movies sell because we love to see the villain caught in the end. Justice can be neatly written into a screenplay. We buy tickets because the passion for resolution in our own lives is vicariously, (though only momentarily), satisfied.

God is not fictitiously written into the screenplay of history. He rights wrongs, corrects inequities, and brings justice in His perfect time. Always.

Your response to the injustice you will encounter *today* will instantly reveal whether or not you really believe this about Him.

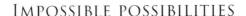

IMPOSSIBLE POSSIBILITIES

" You feed them."

(MATTHEW 14:16)

THE BIBLE IS not given to merely enlarge our intellect, but to change our lives. God intends to bring us to a totally different orientation for living: the way of faith. Account after account is given in the Word to illustrate to us this Godward path we are to follow in every situation of life—to train us so we may learn that "man does not live by bread alone, but by every word that proceeds from the mouth of God" (Matthew 4:4).

He has distinct ways and is gracious to let us know this Divine operating system. And it always begins with an overwhelming need. Scan history and you will see this. Noah faces the impossibility of building an ark and Abraham of sacrificing his only son. Elijah stands before 450 prophets of Baal and David before a 9-foot tall giant.

Each of these men, (and every follower of God, including you), is consistently confronted with impossible situations beyond their ability to navigate. Each encounters the dilemma of faith and must make a choice: *"Will I ignore this clear God-opportunity and try to accomplish this in my own strength, or will I trust God to do the impossible?"*

OUR DAILY TRAINING

One of the most fascinating studies in faith is to watch the unfolding discipling of the twelve by the Master Discipler. It was always about this lesson. At every turn of each day He confronts them with faith dilemmas. Christ interrupts normal moments in which, heretofore, these men would see no God-orientation. He then proceeds to call them to the impossible through the vehicle of belief.

Before these fledgling Christ-followers were 5,000 men and their wives and children. It could have been upward of 20,000 people, but if it had been 200 it would have been just as daunting. It was past dinnertime and all the disciples could muster was a borrowed lunch of five loaves and two fish. The obvious answer to this mathematical equation, (the one which any normal man would propose), was to send them away hungry. But this is not the way God sees life. And people who look through His eyes will not miss these opportunities either.

Christ turns to His disciples and hits them squarely in the face with their spiritual responsibility: *"You feed them."* Can you imagine how ludicrous that must have sounded to these men? How silly? How impossible? But they were about to receive one more lesson in "How a True Believer Lives and Glorifies God."

THE UNCOMMON LESSON

Jesus, as a man, takes what He has, calls out to the Father for His supernatural blessing, and does the impossible. This stunning, but simple act of faith was designed to teach His followers in every age several lessons:

1. **You are responsible to meet the needs of people.** *"You give them something to eat." (Matthew 14:16)*
2. **You cannot do this in your own strength.** *"We have only five loaves here and two fish." (Vs. 17)*
3. **You must take what you have and surrender it fully to God.** *And He said, "Bring them here to me." (Vs. 18)*
4. **You must rely on God to do the impossible—to take what you give Him, bless it, break it, and feed people in ways that astound them (and you) with God's ability and provision.** *Taking the loaves and the two fish, he looked up to heaven and blessed them . . . and broke the loaves and gave them to the disciples and the disciples gave them to the crowds. (Vs. 19)*
5. **You must walk in faith in ways that channel God's overwhelming supply to man's overwhelming need.** *And they all ate and were satisfied. And they took up twelve baskets full of the broken pieces left over. (Vs. 20)*

You may think that the hunger of the people in front of you today is just a human dilemma. In fact, you may shake your head in discouragement at the massive needs you encounter. Overwhelming needs. Impossible needs. If you see it as a merely natural moment of need, you will respond with a natural solution. You will assume there is nothing you can do, and send them away starving.

God wants to feed hungry people through you. But the only way this will ever happen, (and it *can* happen), is if God finds in you a *believer*—a man or woman who is looking for ways to prove God to the hungry crowds through faith. One who sees the impossible as possible and trusts God to deliver in supernatural ways.

You feed them.

DAY 10

FEAR AND FAITH

IF WE ARE to make progress in God we must understand ourselves better. We should realize that our natural propensity is almost always fear. We fear what people think, what will happen in the future, if we have enough in ourselves to accomplish a given task, if we will have the provisions we need—the list is endless.

We are fear experts.

CHRIST'S CALL TO FAITH

When a difficult moment comes, we are especially prone to this debilitating disease. Fear paralyzes us. In Mark, Chapter 5, we have the account of a man whose daughter has died. He comes to Jesus to see if the Great Physician can do anything about his loss. Jesus' response is a classic word that we should etch forever on our minds. It is a word for every occasion for us.

"Do not fear, only believe." (Mark 5:36 ESV)

Faith obliterates fear. This faith that Jesus was calling this father to was not based on a wild, random thought picked out of the blue. It was faith based on the word that Jesus had given. All faith that is true is based on the word of God for "faith comes by hearing and hearing by the word of God" (Romans 10:17).

When we are fearful, our first response should be to get into a position to hear God's evaluation and direction for the situation. Many have opinions for us, but only Christ's voice can generate the kind of faith that pleases God and releases His activity.

THE WORLD'S CALL TO FEAR

We must press out all other voices. Notice that there were some who said, "Don't bother Jesus, your daughter is already dead." There were others who laughed at Jesus even approaching the daughter. Such voices are loud, and if we are not careful they will sweep us right out of faith. But the father climbed up on top of Christ's word and sat down in faith. "Do not fear, only believe," and the results were stunning.

His faith led him to keep following Jesus as they passed the ridiculing crowd and went right to the lifeless daughter's bedside. Something beyond his imagination occurred as Jesus raised the believing father's daughter from the dead. This silenced the mockers, as they were "completely astounded" (Mark 5:42).

If the father had not followed Jesus in faith, would his daughter have been healed? No one knows, but in the very next chapter the scripture records the unbelief of Jesus' hometown citizens and that, "He could do no miracles there … and He wondered at their unbelief" (Mark 6:5-6a).

ARE YOU FEARFUL?

Where is it today that you need to hear and heed Christ's admonition, "Do not fear, only believe"? Something in your work or ministry? Your family? Your finances? A small piranha of fear that is nibbling away your faith or a whale of a problem?

Where is it in your city that God wants to shut the mouth of the mockers and astound the scorners? Could it be that Christ is waiting on you to believe and follow Him before He will release those things that will astound the crowd, bring the dead to life, and bring Him glory?

DAY 11

———— ❦ ————

THE CRITICAL KNOWLEDGE FOR A LEADER

AS A LEADER I have often told the men I work with there's one thing I really don't want them to do: *Don't surprise me!* It puts me at a severe disadvantage if I am caught off guard about some plan they've developed, problem they've encountered, or decision they've made of which I'm unaware.

I have no desire to micro-manage their work, (that's why we've hired them). But I do want to be sufficiently informed about things I need to know about so we can work well together as a team and lead our people effectively.

JESUS' KNOWLEDGE

How can you be a man who knows everything he needs to know, when you need to know it? Jesus was facing Calvary. He had spent the night in the Garden of Gethsemane communing with His Father. In fact, Jesus prayed without ceasing. He was in constant communication with His Father. He needed this because he had laid aside His omniscience and was functioning purely as a human.

Because of this Gethsemane conversation, when the soldiers came to take him to his death, he was not surprised.

Then Jesus, knowing all that would happen to him, came forward" (John 18:4)

How in the world did Christ know "all that would happen to him"?

Prayer.

Apparently the Father knew that His Son needed to be armed with this information to function effectively and so, like the perfect Father He is, He told him at exactly the needed time.

The beauty of this knowledge is seen in Jesus' response. When faced with the most frightening, debilitating moment of His life, Jesus was not in the least afraid or taken aback. He was not flustered or worried. Instead of running or hiding from this challenge or defending Himself, the Bible records He "came *forward.*" No retreat, but a calm embracing of this next chapter of His life. He was in faith.

Why? Because He knew.

When Christ lived on earth He chose to lay aside His rights as God. This means He didn't know everything automatically. As a child, for instance, He had to "*grow* in wisdom" (Luke 2:52). When speaking of the end of the world, He said, "But of that day or hour no one knows, not even the angels in heaven, nor the Son, but the Father alone" (Mark 13:32).

In his manhood, Jesus illustrated that He did not know everything, but he knew everything he needed to know when He needed to know it. And so can we.

MISSING PIECES

Every leader makes the decision every day if he is going to lead out of his own limited knowledge or God's. Will he go forward with his plans or the Father's? I'm not to judge, but it seems to me that most of us pray very little and spend a very small percentage of our time daily in the study of God's Word. We make lots of plans and choices. But do we commune with God enough so that He can tell us all we need to know to move forward successfully in faith? Do we miss God's timing? Abort His direction? Do we ignore His subtle prompting to take time, to pray, to fast, to read, to study, to listen?

If I find myself in a situation that I am so surprised that I am fearful, worried, immobilized, or retreating, it may be that the culprit is my lack of listening. God knows what I need to walk in faith and will always provide the needed instruction if I am paying attention.

I wonder if there's something coming tomorrow that God needs to prepare you for today, so that you can "come *forward*" in faith?

All the more

*But he cried out all the more,
"Son of David, have mercy on me!"*

(Mark 10:48)

WE LIVE IN a wicked day. Divorce is at an all time high. Everyone knows some child that is struggling from the effects of a broken family. Moral impurity, pornography, and adultery are not even considered evil. Materialism and debt—both individual and collective—spiral as we spend what God gives us on ourselves. Almost as an afterthought, we are killing millions of babies every year with a blindness that is staggering.

What can we do? Is it possible to see a reversal of this spiritual and moral trajectory?

CRYING OUT

The Bible often records an interesting and important phrase from God's people when confronted by the discipline and judgment of God: "And all the people cried out to the Lord." You will notice that God always answers a humble cry. Always.

In fact, you could often say that His activity generates that cry just so He can answer in miraculous displays of mercy. Such desperate cries are a part of God's faith equation.

The Gospel of Mark, Chapter 10, records a blind beggar named Bartimaeus who was ridiculed for his uncouth cry to Jesus. His response? He cried out "all the more." The reason was his desperation. Nothing else worked and nothing else mattered. He didn't care what others thought. He was blind. He needed Jesus. He believed Christ was his only hope ... and he would not be refused when Jesus was so near.

Though others rebuked him, Jesus identified his crying as faith. And Christ always responds to faith. Christ stopped. He listened. He responded. He healed. In an amazingly simple, brief moment, a life-long blind beggar became a rejoicing, healed believer. It took very little effort for Christ. It never does for omnipotence.

OUR BLINDNESS AND OUR CRY

Could God send sweeping, national revival to our land? Is it possible for Him to reverse the trends? Many of us have prayed and cried out for years. We wonder if our prayers are making a difference—if God is hearing. If we cried out *all the more* in extraordinary prayer and genuine faith, could He— would He—hear and answer?

Bartimeaus teaches us today. We must not be refused, even when others ridicule us and surge forward with yet another political, social, or even religious plan to reverse the national trends. We must remember that God's mercy is our only hope and the reviving of the church and spiritual awakening of the lost is our only answer.

We must continue in the daily work of the church, but add to our faith the daily cry for a nation-wide movement of God's manifest presence. We must remember that God can transform whole nations as easily as He did a blind beggar beside a dusty, Judean road.

DAY 13

HOW TO ALWAYS MAKE THE
RIGHT DECISIONS

LIFE IS NOTHING less than a series of daily choices. "You are fast becoming what you will one day be," one man said, and that fast track happens one decision at a time.

How can we be assured we're not missing it? That we're making the right choices?

Jesus was right all the time. One of the purposes God had in letting us see Jesus in the flesh was to learn about this decision-making process that can build us into godly men and women.

The difference between Christ and us, obviously, is His perfection. But He intends for us to move more and more into right decision-making as we mature into His likeness. So how do I make choices like Jesus?

START AT THE RIGHT SOURCE

"I can do nothing on my own initiative." (John 5:30)

Jesus, as a man, lived in absolute dependence on the Father. He knew that his earthly life would not be successful if he operated merely on his own. And so, everything He did was at God's initiation. And the mark of a godly man is that he does the same.

Our job is to look up to the Father and let Him initiate— all the time. If you don't humbly embrace this and consistently begin at this ignition point you will not end right. If you initiate the decision, it is bound for failure. But how is this accomplished practically?

LOOK AND LISTEN

> *"The Son can do nothing on his own initiation, but only what he SEES the Father doing." (John 5:19)*

> *"As I HEAR I judge." (John 5:30)*

Jesus was in constant, unceasing communion with God. He was looking into heaven, listening to the Father. Paul emphasizes this same lifestyle when he reminds us we must "pray without ceasing" (1 Thessalonians 5:17).

Jesus was unceasingly watching and listening for the slightest instructions from the Father. Once received, He would simply do everything He saw and heard from Him. No deviation. No additions. No questions. No resistance. Listen and obey.

We are to do exactly the same. To make the right decisions we must be continually looking and listening through the Word of God and prayer and then instantly, explicitly doing what the Father directs.

WITH ONE DESIRE

"I do not seek My own will but the will of Him who sent Me." *(John 5:30)*

One of the primary reasons Christ always made the right decisions is that there was purity in his motivations. No selfish desire for fame, reputation, comfort, self-advancement, or self-glory. It was all about what God desired. "Father what do You want?" was His constant, genuine cry.

Purity in our motivations is a lifelong battle.

We must recognize the constant whispers of the world, the flesh, and the devil pushing us to selfish ambition. As we ruthlessly purify our motivations through the conviction of God's word and time in His presence, we will deal less and less with peripheral ideas, thoughts, and attractions. God's voice will not be clouded by competing noise. Clarity will come and we will gladly choose His way.

Do you want to walk in faith in each decision, trusting God and moving at His initiation? Start at the right source, take the right posture, and live for the right passion.

THE SUFFICIENCY OF DAILY GRACE

"Therefore do not be anxious for tomorrow, for
tomorrow will care for itself.
Each day has enough trouble of its own."

(MATTHEW 6:34)

MOST OF MY trouble is *tomorrow.*

- I don't have enough money for *tomorrow.*
- I have a tough conversation *tomorrow.*
- I've got too much to do *tomorrow.*
- I don't know if I have what it takes for *tomorrow.*
- Things could go really bad *tomorrow.*
- What will people think of me *tomorrow?*

I wallowed in worry recently. Like a heavy comforter, I pulled it up to my chin then right over my head. I don't know why, but it was just there and oppressive. Dark days and sleepless nights spun me in a downward spiral and I just couldn't pull out. I tried to put on a nice face, but nothing was right.

Random personal and family problems nipped at my heels. The "what ifs" of work and ministry burdened my soul. The weight of responsibilities seemed unfairly disproportionate to my strength. Nothing, and I mean nothing, seemed good.

I was angry and short with my family. Usually fairly content, I was upset with God about all the ways I felt He was not coming through on my behalf. Usually fairly trusting, I was suspicious of those around me. What was their agenda? Why was everyone on my back? Nothing seemed to satisfy me.

I looked for comfort in people, things, mindless entertainment. Everything was tasteless. And I felt very, very, very tired.

TOMORROWLAND

Future worry is overwhelming. There's a reason. We don't have grace today for tomorrow. One of Satan's simplest tricks and most effective devices is to draw our attention to things we can do nothing about. There's nothing worse than a crisis that can't be fixed.

If our hours are spent with thoughts of tomorrow's problems, which are not accessible today and which we know we cannot touch with today's resources, we are doomed to worry. And worry wears us out. Worry is the antithesis of faith and a poor testimony to those around us. Those who are not accessing grace are good at worry and deficient at faith.

DAILY GRACE

By faith, Jesus lived in daily grace. He moved with an effortless contentment in the hour. His one preoccupation was to listen to the Father and do what He initiated in the moment. There was sufficient grace for each day. And in quiet trust He believed there would be ample grace for the future.

That's why a "Give us *this day* our *daily* bread" prayer was enough for Him and great instruction for us. Were there massive responsibilities, overwhelming odds, and great enemies ahead for Christ? Seemingly impossible tasks to accomplish with too little time? Nothing more than the salvation of the world, the launching of the church, and the direct onslaughts of the greatest Enemy in eternity! But in light of it all there was uncanny serenity in His daily movements. The contrast to everyone else's life intrigued his friends and unnerved his enemies.

Our calling is today. It's not that we don't think of tomorrow, but it must consistently be filed by faith under "future grace." The tide of confidence in God's sufficiency must wash out worry. In fact, it's a command. "Do not be anxious for tomorrow." To go there is to disobey a directive from the One who holds every moment in His hand.

Live in the sufficiency of daily grace. You need the rest and the world needs the testimony.

THE MOST IMPORTANT QUESTION IN YOUR LIFE RIGHT NOW

*Now on one of those days Jesus and His disciples got
into a boat, and He said to them, "Let us go over to
the other side of the lake." So they launched out.
But as they were sailing along He fell asleep; and
a fierce gale of wind descended on the lake, and
they began to be swamped and to be in danger.
They came to Jesus and woke Him up, saying,
"Master, Master, we are perishing!" And He got
up and rebuked the wind and the surging waves,
and they stopped, and it became calm. And He
said to them,*
"Where is your faith?"
*They were fearful and amazed, saying to one an-
other, "Who then is this, that He commands even
the winds and the water, and they obey Him?"*

(LUKE 8:22-24)

GOD HAS ONE primary system with man and He needs only
one. The Garden led man to independence; God's whole
agenda is to bring us back to dependence ... to faith in Him.

At each and every turn of our lives this is the issue. Ten thousand times He is asking us, "Where is your faith? Are you going to believe me or not? Depend upon Me or your human logic and meager resources? Trust in My promises or wallow in self-pity and anxiety?"

IT'S PERSONAL

This question was extremely individual for every man in the storm. They had to answer for themselves. If twelve individuals believed, it would have led to great strength in the whole. But still, each man had to look into the gracious, clear eyes of Jesus and answer His question: "Where is *your* faith?"

Those eyes look inside our soul every day. With a burden to build us up, they search the depths of our heart to see the level of our trust. Jesus looks for increasing maturity in our dependence.

This is why the tests come at increasing levels. He intends us to become larger conduits for His glory and also greater knowers of Him. Each step of faith and His corresponding faithfulness make us not only more useful, but better equipped.

If you are a leader He knows your role must be uniquely characterized by faith. All of us lead and influence someone. Jesus has designed us to lead in dependence and passion, and so His training for leaders is more rigorous. Don't resist this as a hindrance, but welcome it as a signal of God's unique confidence in you.

In the midst

If you are troubled right now, or anxious, or besieged with doubts and fears, or feeling strangely out of sorts, the remedy is not the release from your storm. Jesus was sleeping in the midst of the turmoil. He was illustrating that rest comes from confidence in the Father. He knew that God had Him covered and that there was a path for His life that would not be thwarted by a mere earthly disturbance. Faith gave Him rest.

In reality, faith is most beautiful in the midst of a raging storm. Like a light that takes on extraordinary brilliance in the darkest room, faith is most useful and most visible in troubled seasons.

If you are fearful or worried right now, anxious about this or that, check your faith. You will find that lurking unbelief is always the culprit, sneaking in to rob you of your rest.

LEARNING FROM

THE HEROES OF OUR FAITH

DAY 16

IMITATABLE FAITH

Remember your leaders, those who spoke to you the word of God.
Consider the outcome of their way of life, and imitate their faith.

(HEBREWS 13:7)

WE ALL HAVE heroes. It's tragic that often the world defines this for us in ways that are less than best. We follow people who are athletically gifted, politically persuasive, those who have business savvy, or are full of entertainment attraction. They are known for certain things that set them apart.

As spiritual leaders—in our home, ministry, church, community—we should be known for something too. But there is one quality that should mark us above all else: *faith.* We should be heroes of belief. Men and women of dependency and expectancy. People of extraordinary trust.

FAITH'S BENEFITS
If we truly walk in faith there are "outcomes" of this "way of life" that make others desire to follow us into such a life.

The more we walk in faith, the more God is in the equation. The more God is in the equation, the more He is seen for the mighty God He is. And the more He is seen, the more people are drawn to Him and He is worshipped. And when, by faith, we have been so used, we have accomplished the great business of heaven and earth. We have a way of life worth imitating.

The leaders that the writer of Hebrews speaks of imitating are those who "spoke to you the word of God." There is a technical sense in which he is speaking here of pastors and teachers, but the reality is that any leader who is full of faith will be speaking God's Word into the lives of those who follow. The Lord, as he leads them, will see to that. This presupposes then, that a man of faith is a man who has heard from God, believes God, and speaks God's word to others.

SOME FAITH QUESTIONS

So how do I become a hero of imitatable faith? Here are six questions to help you evaluate and move forward in belief.

1. *Am I hearing God through His Word?*
2. *Am I responding instantly to what He says in growing, vibrant, risk-taking faith?*
3. *Is this a "way of life" with me, or just intermittent crisis moments along the way?*
4. *Am I seeing "outcomes" of faith through my life that make others long to have this faith-life? Is there faith-fruit?*

5. *Would others say that the single most recognizable quality of my life is that I am man or woman of faith? One who depends on God alone in each situation, hears from Him, and then lives obediently as if what God says is really true?*
6. *Am I at rest?*

If these questions trouble you, ask God to do whatever necessary to increase your faith quotient. Study His Word to hear from Him and receive His next assignment. When He speaks, trust Him and obey, *and keep trusting until you die.*

DAY 17

PREPARATORY FAITH
Or, "Lions, and Tigers, and Bears, Oh my!"

*And Saul said to David, "You are not able to go
against this Philistine to fight with him, for you
are but a youth, and he has been a man of war
from his youth."
But David said to Saul, "Your servant used to keep
sheep for his father. And when there came a lion,
or a bear, and took a lamb from the flock, I went
after him and struck him and delivered it out of his
mouth. And if he arose against me, I caught him by
his beard and struck him and killed him. Your servant has struck down both lions and bears, and this
uncircumcised Philistine shall be like one of them, for
he has defied the armies of the living God."
And David said, "The Lord who delivered me from
the paw of the lion and from the paw of the bear
will deliver me from the hand of this Philistine."
And Saul said to David, "Go, and the Lord be
with you!"*

(1 SAMUEL 17:33-37)

When was the last time you faced a giant in battle? Not the "9-foot-tall-Goliath" kind, but the "I-have-a-problem-that-is-overwhelming" kind?

Each challenge, big or small, is an exercise to help you decide who you will depend upon—who you will trust. God, in His patient wisdom, builds this faith one circumstance at a time. He gives us bite-sized issues that He knows our faith can negotiate by His grace. Any faith challenge is a stretch to our belief or it would not call for faith. Day-by-day and challenge-by-challenge, He builds our capacity for greater faith and thus, greater usefulness.

Our daily, progressive training

Young David probably thought his whole life would be spent on the backside of a Bethlehem pasture tending sheep, which was the lot of most young men of his day. But this was merely a temporary, hillside seminary. He was in a training that he did not realize, as all of us are. God allowed lions and bears to cross the young shepherd's path on purpose. At each turn he stood and faced these trials depending upon a greater Strength. He recognized that it was the "Lord who delivered me from the paw of the lion and from the paw of the bear."

Imagine those encounters! His enemies were huge. He probably thought he would never experience any bigger challenges—that these were the greatest life stories he would tell. But it was all preparation. Little did David realize that he was in boot camp. He was learning how to trust God and face enemies. How to be instantly decisive in faith. How to hear from God and act upon His initiation. How to believe God in the moment for His enabling.

Before he knew it and certainly before anyone around him dreamed he was ready, his enemies would have human faces. When the time came, he was spiritually prepared. His faith was at the place of such absolute confidence that a 9-foot giant seemed like one more lion. With absolute faith he believed that "the Lord will deliver me from the hand of this Philistine." This giant was simply the next test in his lifelong training. No one else that day was as spiritually ready as young David. He had been equipped by fully trusting the Chief Shepherd on the hillsides, day after day.

LIONS AND TIGERS AND BEARS, OH MY!

What are the enemies and difficulties God is allowing in your life right now? They seem massive—the biggest, most all-consuming challenges of your life. But the issue is never the size of your problem but the size of your God and your willingness to believe.

Will you turn to God? Will you rely on your own limited intellect to work out the equation? Will you worry it to death? Will you bear down with intensity to try to control and manipulate by your own devices? Will you lay in bed night after night gripped with speculation and fear? Will you allow the enemy to run roughshod over you and overpower your spiritual life?

Or, will you turn to the Father? Will you rely on His wisdom and get your instruction and promise from His word? Will you rest and wait patiently for Him? Will you move forward in belief, trusting in God's complete sufficiency? And, will you let these initial battles prepare you for your life's work?

The endgame with God is always about others' good and His glory. His plan for David was to use him mightily to help build God's kingdom in ways that a self-dependent Saul could not do. God needed a man after His own heart. A man who would trust and obey. A man who would grow with each test and become humbly emboldened with deepening convictions.

And lest you think that this preparation is only for the young, remember that David's hardest challenges were in his later years. You can never relax or imagine that any issue is not about faith. Just when you think you can retire from spiritual development, God faces you with the next giant. This is because our earthly years are miniscule compared to what God is readying us for in the eons of eternity.

We must embrace the reality that our training always extends—lions and tigers and bears till death—continually preparing us for greater experiences of eternal usefulness.

THE NECESSARY PREPARATION
FOR OUR MOST IMPORTANT JOB

WORSHIP IS OUR main calling and occupation. It is the highest form of human activity and should never be thought of merely in terms of a Sunday morning experience. It is our responses to God that give Him worth and dominion and honor through our lives, and should be participated in 24 hours a day. It is seeing God as He is and giving Him what He deserves.

But what precedes worship? Why do some people worship and others don't?

And the people believed; and when they heard that the Lord had visited the people of Israel and that he had seen their affliction, they bowed their heads and worshiped. (Exodus 4:31 ESV)

BELIEF FOSTERS WORSHIP

When we see some of the activity of God and believe in Him, it stimulates awe and leads us to give Him the honor that He deserves. Genuine faith is the catalyst to worship—the necessary driver. If we do not believe, we will never turn to

Him in conscious praise and adoration. Unbelief leads to self-worship and a life that leaves God completely out of the equation.

SEEING FOSTERS BELIEF

Do you have a hard time worshipping? Maybe it's because you are not seeing God daily—in nature, in others, in His word, in your own experience—and believing in Him.

To see Him you must look. You are bombarded with thousands of images and noises everyday and seeing God is not automatic. "He is there and He is not silent," as Frances Schaeffer said, but we must realize that our enemy has designed distractions galore. To see takes intentionality and spiritual focus.

But to see is to believe and to believe is to worship. If we fail in this task we instinctively slide down a slippery slope, and "worship and serve the creature instead of the Creator (Romans 1:25)."

If you want to lead people to worship, walk in deep faith so that God is released in and through and around you. People will "stand amazed in the presence of Jesus, the Nazarene," and sing a new song to Him.

DAY 19

❦

AN INCOMPLETE RECIPE

HAVE YOU EVER ventured into the cooking world as a man, thought you had done an exceptional job on a batch of cookies, but realized sadly that you'd left out the most important ingredient? As men, we need to learn to stay on our side of the line!

The writer of Hebrews reminds us of a more critical failure: to fail to add FAITH to what God has said to us. The most vivid illustration to the Hebrews was their ancestors who could have walked into the Promised Land 40 years earlier, but they wandered in the wilderness and died simply because they would not depend upon God. They lacked the ingredient of faith.

> *For good news came to us just as to them, but the message they heard did not benefit them, because they were not united by faith with those who listened. (Hebrews 4:2)*

IT'S PERSONAL

This illustration is not just ancient history, but a reminder that "good news came to us just as to them." In other words, God is speaking all the time through His Word and by His Spirit to you personally. He is telling you what to do and challenging you to trust Him and move forward in believing faith. You have the first ingredient, (God's word to you), but if you don't add in faith the whole cake collapses.

A.W. Tozer said the great tragedy of our American Christianity is thinking that because we know something we have it. God has spoken to you about your family, your time, your money, your giving, your ministry and on and on. In His word you have "everything pertaining to life and godliness." But are you embracing what He says and acting on it?

IT'S OBEDIENCE

Faith is a verb. Noah BUILT an ark. Abraham WENT OUT to a strange land, Moses CHOOSE to endure ill treatment with God's people over the passing pleasures of sin. They heard what God said and responded in faith by walking and talking like what God said was really true. It was this final ingredient of obedience that illustrated they really believed, made room for God, and brought Him right into the action of their daily lives.

As spiritual leaders, this is even more critical for us. Our faith, or lack thereof, affects everyone we are responsible to lead. Of all people we must be pioneers of obedient faith in every arena of our lives. It comes with the territory and is our most powerful leadership tool.

What has God said to you right now? The next ingredient that He is asking you to add that proves His ability and reflects on His glory? Stir in obedient faith and feed the world.

BACKING UP ON GOD

IT'S EASY. IN fact, "natural" would be a good word. It is entirely possible for a follower of Christ to pull away from his previous faith and back up on God.

A SOBERING REMINDER

King Asa was a great leader who had been used of God to rout an army twice his size through the artillery of faith (see 2 Chronicles 15). But, when faced with a new challenge he returned to the natural path of independent thinking.

> At that time Hanani the seer came to Asa king of Judah and said to him, "Because you relied on the king of Syria, and did not rely on the Lord your God, the army of the king of Syria has escaped you. Were not the Ethiopians and the Libyans a huge army with very many chariots and horsemen? Yet because you relied on the Lord, he gave them into your hand. For the eyes of the Lord run to and fro throughout the whole earth, to give strong support to those whose heart is blameless toward him. You have done foolishly in this, for from now on you will have wars." (2 Chronicles 16:7-9)

It seems so foolish, doesn't it, when we look back at someone like Asa from the lens of history? But I wonder what our unbelief looks like? How often has God cornered us with impossible odds just to display His glory and we have backed away from full faith?

The most tragic thing was Asa's response when confronted. Instead of repentance, (like David with Nathan the prophet when challenged with his sin), Asa shoots the messenger.

> *Then Asa was angry with the seer and put him in the stocks in prison, for he was in a rage with him because of this. And Asa inflicted cruelties upon some of the people at the same time. (2 Chronicles 16:10)*

The Bible records further that Asa persisted in his ways.

> *In the thirty-ninth year of his reign Asa was diseased in his feet, and his disease became severe. Yet even in his disease he did not seek the Lord, but sought help from physicians. (2 Chronicles 16:12)*

We all make mistakes, and God is not demanding perfection. But He longs for us to live as He designed and knows that anything less is detrimental to others and ourselves. If we've backed up we need to kneel down, and quickly.

DAY 21

—— ❧ ——

BELIEVING THE UNSEEN

FAITH IS THE initial, continuing, and eternal agenda of God. It is through faith that we enter into a relationship with Christ and through faith that we operate in that relationship. It is the primary foundation for our communion with our Creator.

FAITH'S DEFINITION
Now faith is the assurance of things hoped for, the conviction of things not seen. (Hebrews 11:1)

Faith begins by hearing from the Lord. When we hear God's word to us—about life in general or a specific issue—the question is, "Will we believe Him? Will we depend on Him alone? Will we re-orient our life on the basis of this conviction? Will we make every necessary adjustment that real faith demands?"

When faith is present it brings something mighty to us: the assurance that we will experience what we hope for and the conviction that what is not seen is a genuine reality.

No one can drum up this belief. You cannot manufacture it or act like it's there when God has given you no basis for faith. Many people try to believe without hearing from God. They stir their emotions into a lather and say, "It is so" when it is not so. This is not faith, but mere presumption and will yield no lasting fruit. In fact, it can cause great damage to others who may be weak in faith.

ABUNDANT PROMISES

Most of the promises that engender faith are the simple, clear, normative statements from God's Word. "Be anxious for nothing, but in everything by prayer and supplication with thanksgiving let your requests be made known to God. And the peace of God, which surpasses all comprehension, will guard your hearts and your minds in Christ Jesus" (Philippians 4:6-7). "Seek first the kingdom of God and His righteousness and all these things will be added unto you" (Matthew 6:33). A faithful God spells out over 7,000 such promises in His Word and each promise is forever settled in heaven.

A PERSONAL PROMISE

When my father went through a severe crisis at 65 years of age, my precious Mother began crying out to God on his behalf. The Lord gave her, she believed, the following promise:

> *"Because he has loved Me, therefore I will deliver him; I will set him securely on high, because he has known My name. He will call upon Me, and I will answer him; I will be with*

him in trouble; I will rescue him and honor him. With a long life I will satisfy him and let him see My salvation." *(Psalm 91)*

They were both in their mid-sixties when this tragedy occurred. On my mother's deathbed at 69, she heard my father's voice as he called her to seek forgiveness. God had rescued him and his repentance was deep and lasting.

My father died at 97 years of age, 28 years after my mother's death. He lived a long life and each day thanked God for His redemption. The last few years were the widest expansion of his ministry as he spoke to thousands of pastors in multiple venues telling the story of his fall and God's mercy. He began many of those messages with this statement: *"No man can rise so high that he cannot fall, and no man can fall so low that he cannot rise by the grace of God."*

My mother saw those days by faith 30 years before. Not the particulars, but the reality of God's rescue. She received God's word and it became the conviction of her heart that God would do what He'd promised.

Blessed, life-changing faith. Blessed, restful confidence. Blessed, faithful God!

GOD'S COMPREHENSIVE WORD

IT IS THE sad experience of many Christians that they think of God's Word as an inanimate object. The Bible is simply a book to them. And so, they find themselves treating it like any other piece of literature.

For many it is easily ignored. Long periods of time pass when the Bible is not used, sitting on a shelf like an undiscovered treasure.

CASUAL CONTEMPT

Disregard could be the way to describe how others treat the Word. They may hear it, even reading it for themselves, but they fail to regard it for what it is. They treat it as a common collection of merely wise sayings that they have the option to either obey or neglect at their whim.

But neither of these responses understands the true nature of the Bible. It is GOD'S present Word. God is speaking directly and immediately. It's as if you were sitting at a kitchen table across from Jesus Himself. He is talking to you. Do you think that His communication is not binding? That you will not be judged by how you respond to what He is saying?

He is giving you an opportunity for life and forgiveness and healing and usefulness at every sentence. If you chose not to respond to His immediate words, you will experience all that a life not directed by God affords—unforgiveness, guilt, shame, uselessness—and the list goes on. He has come to give us life, and that abundantly. Surely we understand the alternative is death? How else is this accessed but by listening intently, honoring fully, and adjusting our lives immediately to what He is saying?

THE WORD WE BELIEVE

When the writer of Hebrews, under Divine inspiration, expressed the nature of God's word, he said,

> *For the word of God is living and active, sharper than any two-edged sword, piercing to the division of soul and of spirit, of joints and of marrow, and discerning the thoughts and intentions of the heart. And no creature is hidden from his sight, but all are naked and exposed to the eyes of him to whom we must give account. (Hebrews 4:12-13)*

Think of these words, particularly in regard to how you currently treat the Bible. God's word is...

- **Living**. It is not static, but as real and alive as what you might say. But more than human conversation, it gives life to all those who chose to receive it.

- **Active**. It does things. When God speaks, mountains are lifted up and seas are created. People's lives are taken from hell to heaven.
- **Sharper than a two-edged sword.** Notice it is not "as sharp" but "sharper." Think of the sharpest double-edged sword you can imagine, cutting both coming and going. God's word is more divisive than that. It cuts. It can slice through hypocrisy, and foolishness—through our sin and excuses and the fog of confused thinking. It can cut through a crowd that is oblivious to Him and expose their hearts in an instant.
- **Piercing to the division of both soul and spirit.** His word immediately dissects between what is soulish, carnal, fleshly, and that which is of the Spirit. A man may be saying with merely human opinion, "This is God's will," and when a simple verse of Scripture is quoted it exposes that what he is saying is completely of the flesh, not the Spirit.
- **Discerning the thoughts and intentions of the heart.** The Bible goes deeper than any Damascus steel blade. His word not only uncovers our true thoughts, but pierces to the bedrock of our motivations.

You can ignore the Word or play games with it, but the final sentence is the most telling. The Word of God exposes us. This is not a terrible thing, but terribly *helpful*. Without this exposure we can go along blindly, completely in the dark about our real condition.

The prophet said that God's Word is like an anvil. Unchanging, strong. You do not break an anvil. Everything is broken upon it. "Forever, O, Lord, Thy word is settled in heaven," is a wonderful statement of the unchangeableness of God. He is always the same and we can trust that the promises He made thousands of years ago are just as alive and active today.

God is speaking. He is across the table from you right now saying exactly what you need to hear. Are you listening and responding in faith?

DAY 23

———— ✥ ————

ARE YOU REFUSING?

See that you do not refuse him who is speaking.

(HEBREWS 11:26)

GOD IS SPEAKING all the time. It is His primary way to be known. He has chosen to reveal Himself so that we can known Him better and love Him more. Through creation, conscience, Christ, His Word and His Spirit, every day is filled with His voice. His line has gone out to the ends of the earth. Where can we hide from His Spirit?

HIS PURPOSEFUL VOICE

This is not just a Divine mechanical process because God knows it must work this way. It was His passion from the beginning. He loves His family. Really loves us. He longs for us, wants to talk with us, and cherishes our time together.

And He cares about our every step. You might say to God, "I didn't think you'd care what I did," or, "I thought your only interest was to supervise or reprimand me," but you would be wrong. He wants companionship, not just obedience. When

He speaks it is to help you, guide you, encourage you more than your greatest friend. It is not just His *words* He wants you to interact with, but *Him*.

OUR THOUGHTLESS REJECTION

Being refused when you are initiating a relationship feels awful. Talk to those who have gone through the leaving of a spouse. They will tell you that it is worse than death. Death of one you are deeply connected to is excruciating, but it is natural, understandable, explainable.

When a spouse elects to leave you, the loss and loneliness must be dealt with, but there is the additional pain of rejection—the worst human emotion.

Notice that the admonition of this verse in Hebrews is not about rejecting God's words, but rejecting Him. "Do not refuse HIM who is speaking."

God is not like us. His emotions are perfect and His understanding is complete. But He still calls us to not refuse Him. He knows it is not good for either party. His words to us form the foundation of faith and "without faith it is impossible to please God" (Hebrews 11:6a)

When we fail to fully respond to this perfect Father it always leads to disaster. God longs to protect us from this because He loves us. Each time we listen and embrace what He is saying, we come to know Him more and love and trust Him better.

SELECTIVE HEARING

Many of us in Christianity have the amazing ability to act like we're hearing something, even parrot it back, but then allow it to have no effect on our lives. We are adept at this hypocrisy. We are hearing with our ears and even some of our mind, but not responding to what we hear or to the one who is speaking.

When we do this with God, it is a deadly practice that practically and emotionally distances us from the One who loves us. Oft repeated it creates a pseudo-relationship that coats our conscience momentarily, but does nothing to change our lives or cement our connection with the Father.

We are refusing what God is saying, but more foundationally, we are rejecting an intimate relationship with the only One who loves us in the way our soul desires. If we ignore Him, as one man has said, our "souls will go in silent search of other lovers."

DAY 24

THE DAILY RELEVANCE OF GOD'S WORD

*"By You I can run a troop and by my God I can
leap over a wall"*

(PSALM 18:29)

GOD SPEAKS. THERE is no question that God's great intention
is to have a relationship with His creation that includes personal conversation. This is an amazing condescension on his
part and the greatest opportunity on ours.

Those who view Him and His Word, the Bible, as a static book have missed what makes Christianity so amazingly
real. He said Himself that His word is "alive and powerful"
(Hebrews 4:12). Because its author is God, anything is possible. And because He has given those who know Him His
Spirit, there is the mind-boggling possibility of picking up
the Bible and having a conversation as if God were sitting
across the table speaking in an audible voice, talking to us
about the next moments of our day.

A FAITH-BIRTHING SONG
David, the sweet Psalmist of Israel, and her best king other
than the Messiah, wrote Psalm 18 several thousands years

84

ago. It was intended to be a Psalm read and sung, voiced and experienced by people. It recounts the glorious ability of God to empower us even in the face of our worst enemies. The mere reading of this Psalm, written and spoken to our hearts by the Holy Spirit, births faith and courage as we think of our mighty, defending God.

Early in my ministry, I was so overwhelmed by the magnitude of the task of my first church out of seminary that I almost did not accept the invitation to become their pastor. Debating whether or not I had the right stuff, I went to God's word for an answer. I came to this Psalm and will never forget our conversation.

David said, "By You I can run a troop and by my God I can leap over a wall." The verse immediately birthed God-initiated faith in my heart. I knew that if God could do that for David, he would give me what I needed.

God spoke. I heard. I accepted the call and His grace in me was more than sufficient for the task. I had a direct conversation with God through His word. It was alive. It was real. It directed me. God was my counselor and in humility I embraced His directive and found Him leading me in "all the paths of righteousness for His name's sake." I later understood that this was as much about the process as the end result. God was teaching me how we were to partner together.

ABUSING THE WORD

This process of biblical communication can be abused of course. "Judas went out and hanged himself" is not a direct command to us about our lives, particularly when coupled with the verses, "Go and do thou likewise" and, "What thou doest, do quickly!"

Some claim wild interpretations of God's word. God does speak through the principles learned in Judas' story. It reminds us of the consequences of treachery and the crushing weight of an unclear conscience. All of God's word speaks in its proper context. But when someone abuses the word, twisting it to say what God does not, it does not negate the reality of God's voice to those who humbly seek Him. That abuse tells us more about our sinfulness than His lack of communication.

READY TO TALK

God speaks today. If you don't have His Spirit in you, you will never experience this communion (1 Corinthians 2:6-15). But also, your approach to the Scripture each day is vital. If I simply read the Word as a mere historical document, (which is the revealing term used by liberal theologians), I will experience no Divine conversation.

But if I humbly come, filled with His Spirit, to the living Word of the living God, I will hear Him. He delights to reveal himself with glorious clarity. There is no more compelling, enlightening, engaging voice.

DAY 25

———— ❦ ————

YOUR LEPROSY IS SHOWING
2 KINGS 5

IT'S NOT COMPLICATED. The Creator of the world speaks to us and we are to listen and gladly obey. Sharp attention and prompt obedience indicates our understanding of God's loving authority over our lives and our absolute confidence in His perfect rightness.

THE WALL

But there is a massive barrier to our faith. Pride, which has the ever present "**I**" in the middle. And it's in all of us.

Naaman was a great man in his community, "but he was a leper." Just one little problem with this powerful man: he was dying.

Each of us has the same diagnosis. *"He is the CEO of the company, but he is dying." "She is the coolest girl in school, but she is dying." "He is the wealthiest man in town, but he is dying."* This reality hangs on all of us, physically and spiritually. We are eternally sick and there is nothing on earth or in ourselves than can concoct a cure.

At the prompting of a courageous servant girl, Naaman finds his way to Elisha, the man of God who Naaman thought would wave a magic wand and cure him. He came to Elisha's house and the wise old prophet, led by God's Spirit, would not even come to the door. Elisha was completely unimpressed by Naaman's credentials, but totally impressed by God's. He knew pride when he saw it and God had a beautiful antidote.

PRIDE-BUSTERS

The Commander of Pride was enraged. "Behold **I** thought, he would do what **I** expected in **my** way on **my** terms," he cried. Then Elisha took it one pride-smashing step further, as God always does. He told him to go and wash in the muddy, Hebrew river seven times.

The dying leper had a problem: humble himself, believe God, obey Him explicitly and be healed, or, go home and die in his pride and unbelief. It took an encouraging servant to push him on to faith, (as it often does), and the result was the greatest miracle of God he'd ever experienced.

Where is the leprosy in your life or the lives of those around you who need God's healing? What step has God asked of you that you have resisted? Has God sent a servant to push you to dependence and have you have responded with, "Behold **I** thought," and walked away from a miracle?

He is waiting to do miracles in and through you—things that will astound the world. But your greatest healing may be the elimination of your pride and unbelief.

DAY 26

THE OBEDIENCE OF FAITH

"Paul, a bond-slave of Christ Jesus ...
through whom we have received grace and apostle-
ship to bring about
the obedience of faith among all the Gentiles for
His name's sake."

(ROMANS 1:1A, 5)

CHRISTIANITY IS SLAVERY. In these days of easy belief, some wrongly conclude Christianity is an add-on to life. In a moment of crisis or need they "receive" Christ to give some measure of relief. For many there is no thought of submission to a Master or surrender to a Sovereign King. Bended knees and yielded allegiance is not in their thinking. To Paul, these people may not know Christ at all.

Paul's favorite description of himself was a bond-slave. We know little of this concept, having been delivered from the grotesque human institution of slavery in our nation. But in Paul's world it was everywhere. He witnessed first-hand the chains of servitude. He knew that to be a slave was to have no will of your own. To give up rights and privileges. To be owned by another. Absolute obedience.

And yet, "Paul, a bond-slave of Christ" was his opening introduction to people he didn't even know. He was so convinced of the beauty of this unique, spiritual slavery that it became the goal of his ministry to bring people to the "obedience of faith." To obey is to listen attentively and respond submissively. It is to yield our rights to past, present, and future. To allow Someone else to determine the course of our life.

TRUSTING SUBMISSION

We would choose the benefits of faith as our primary goal. Paul's objective was nothing less than "obedience to the faith" in those he discipled and in his own life. He knew that obedience was the end result of trust. If I trust someone it is not hard to respond to their leadership.

How could Paul so gladly announce his slavery and call others to the same? He knew the Master. "I have found that God is easy to live with," said Tozer, and Paul would agree. Although His demands are unwavering, His grace, love, and provision are astounding.

Not only is God worthy of our obedience, but such obedience is the singular path to freedom. A train is only free when it runs the tracks designed for it. We were designed for God and we operate best when we are in on the tracks designed for us by our Sovereign King.

We would do well to examine our faith. Does the word "obedience" describe your relationship with Him? Do you recoil at that word? If obedience is not a result of glad surrender, your Christianity may be insufficient; a counterfeit of real faith.

DAY 27

THE CONSTANT, GLORIOUS PURPOSE OF OUR CURRENT, GRIEVOUS PROBLEMS

SINCE THE GARDEN, every man and woman has been plagued with a terminal disease related to trust. Our natural, fallen state is self-reliance. Particular "sins" are not the genesis, but the by-product of this independence from God. We persistently think we know better than God what is best for our lives and we live accordingly.

GOD'S RELENTLESS PURSUIT

Our Father, who loves us with an everlasting love, is eternally committed to resolving this problem and bringing us to His side in beautiful dependency. He wants us to experience the tender and powerful position of reliance on Him and Him alone. He knows that any other place is disastrous for those He's created.

Because He's our Creator, He knows the optimum standard-operating-procedure. It can be summed up in a word: TRUST. Unequivocal, humble, constant reliance is His goal. Search the biblical record and you will find it on every page. We call this "faith," "dependence," "believing," but it is all about being pushed back to His side. It is the humble brokenness that realizes He alone has the words of eternal life and the nearness of God is our greatest good.

OUR MATURING FAITH

Paul understood this so well that he viewed all of life from this matured perspective. Such spiritual understanding helps us see our problems and adversaries properly, just as he experienced on his travels in Asia.

> "For we do not want you to be unaware, brothers, of the afflic-
> tion we experienced in Asia. For we were so utterly burdened
> beyond our strength that we despaired of life itself. Indeed, we
> felt that we had received the sentence of death. **But that was
> to make us rely not on ourselves but on God who raises the
> dead.** He delivered us from such a deadly peril, and he will
> deliver us. On him we have set our hope that he will deliver
> us again." (1 Corinthians 1:8-10 ESV, emphasis mine)

God knows our streak of self-reliance is so strong it can only be broken by pressure. It is when we are "utterly burdened beyond our strength" that our pride crumbles like the dry bread it is and we know we must have deeper nourishment. We kick against this process, but this is a good and necessary expression of the Father's love. Without this, we would hope-lessly whirl into a godless life, never seeing our need and turning to trust "God who raises the dead" who alone "will deliver us."

It will save us great worry, frustration, and time if we will come to the settled recognition of the necessity of breaking this self-reliance in our lives. We will be wise to embrace the part that pressure plays in getting and keeping us in faith and that a glorious Love drives us to "despair of life itself … to make us rely not on ourselves but on God."

There is, in reality, no safer or better place to be.

—— ❧ ——

THE ISSUE

IT'S AMAZING WHAT can be learned from the simplest of life experiences. A missed opportunity can teach us about the urgency of life. A financial need can overwhelm us with lessons on provision and our real security. And even a fishing trip can teach us about faith.

Faith is always the issue. It runs through both Old and New Testaments and right up to your front door. For the Apostle Peter, it came right up to the side of his boat.

THE FAITH CALL

Here is Peter, the impetuous, young disciple in Luke, Chapter Five. He is a professional fisherman who knows what He is doing. He has fished all night and caught nothing. But then a Carpenter gives him a Divine word.

"Put out into the deep and let your nets down for a catch," Jesus said to Peter, which seemed absolutely foolish to every sensory perception and all his years of training.

THE FAITH CRISIS

At this point, Peter had what Henry Blackaby calls a "crisis of belief." "Will I trust God—even though it doesn't make sense to me—or not? Will I believe what God has said? Will I operate in the material sphere or the spiritual? And, will I illustrate my faith through instant obedience?"

THE FAITH STEP
Peter passes the test, ("But, at Thy bidding, I will let down the net"). Here was the word of faith, the crisis of faith, and then, the obedience of faith.

Faith always follows this pattern. God tells us something and we must decide whether or not to believe. If we truly believe, it will always be illustrated by a step of obedience to the revealed will of God. Belief without obedience is not real faith. Obedience is the ultimate illustration of dependence.

THE FAITH REWARD
And faith is always rewarded. Peter cast his nets in faith and look what he received:

- **A great catch.** *And when they had done this, they enclosed a large number of fish, and their nets were breaking (Vs. 6).* God is always faithful to do exceedingly abundantly beyond all that we ask or think.
- **A humbled believer.** *When Simon Peter saw it, he fell down at Jesus' knees saying, "Depart from me, for I am a sinful man, O Lord" (Vs. 8).* When we trust, God is released to show Himself. When believers see God's activity it always reminds them of the difference

between the Creator and the creature. Our pride is put in its rightful place.

- **An amazed crowd.** *For he and all who were with him were astonished at the catch of fish that they had taken (Vs.9).* The world will always be amazed when they see the reality and power of God. This is our greatest witness to a watching crowd. Amazement was an oft-repeated word in the ministry of Jesus and the early church. Sadly, it is one of the missing words of the church and most believer's lives today.

God is daily putting us into this position so that we will learn and lean. This is the case in huge steps or the simple response of listening and responding to Him in the midst of a conversation or a fishing trip.

God may be telling you to let down your nets today. Whether or not you see His activity depends on the level of your belief.

DIVINELY INTENTIONAL

GOD NEVER WASTES words. When He prompts you to take a step of faith, there is a reason. Philip, a deacon in the early church, was preaching in Samaria with great results. Many were coming to Christ. But God led him to leave this place of fruitful ministry and go to the desert. He responded with no questions or arguing. He simply, immediately obeyed the Holy Spirit.

> *Now an angel of the Lord said to Philip, "Rise and go toward the south to the road that goes down from Jerusalem to Gaza." This is a desert place. And he rose and went. And there was an Ethiopian, a eunuch, a court official of Candace, queen of the Ethiopians, who was in charge of all her treasure. He had come to Jerusalem to worship. (Acts 8:26-27)*

Philip's seasoned faith paved the way for unquestioning obedience and put him in a perfect environment for usefulness. To some people, where he was sent was a desert to be avoided. For Philip, it was merely the next step of faith in his all-knowing God—a highway to ministry. Surprisingly, it became one of his most important moments of life. And for the Ethiopian eunuch, who was dying of spiritual thirst, it was an eternal oasis in the midst of a barren existence.

Why did this beautiful thing happen, recorded for our instruction? Because God was seeking someone who was seeking Him and God's servant was ready to obey in faith with no questions asked.

DIVINE APPOINTMENTS

This powerful official from another continent, (the first indication that the gospel was spread to Ethiopia), just happened to be reading the scroll of Isaiah as Philip walked up. It just happened to be at a prophetic passage about Jesus. Philip just happened to appear and just happened to be divinely equipped to preach Jesus to him.

The Ethiopian just happened to believe in Jesus as His Savior. And then, there just happened to be a pool of water for this new believer to be baptized. It's amazing what just happens when we trust and obey without reservation!

YOUR NEXT TRIP TO THE DESERT

Our part in the story of others salvation is written by God's grace and our unquestioning obedience. God longs to use you—far more than you realize and far more often than you would expect—if you will listen to the Spirit and go wherever He says (even to a desert). Keep your eyes open and faith current today. Something might *just happen!*

D A Y 3 0

―――――― ⋙⋘ ――――――

CAN GOD REALLY SPEAK TO ME TODAY?

THE CHRISTIAN KINGDOM is filled with imbalance. Someone sees a heresy—a truth out of balance—and then swings so far to the other side that they are equally wrong.

Does God speak to us today? There could be very few questions of greater importance because "faith comes by hearing and hearing by the Word of God." How can anything be more critical than knowing whether or not I can personally commune with the God of the Universe? Ideas on this subject are as abundant as Christians.

But how does He speak? Who is right on this subject: the one who says God never speaks to us now except through His Word, or the one who says God told him to jump off a cliff?

FAITH KILLERS

The purely secular person explains everything in terms of science. Any supposed voice is explained away as natural phenomena.

Many pastors do not go that far, but they confine God's voice to His written Word, believing when the Bible was finalized God's voice was silenced. They explain that the Bible is God's full revelation and there is no more need for another word. They have great reverence for God's authoritative word, (as do I), but give little room for the communication of His Spirit. If they are not careful, they may take the full, spiritual dynamic right out of their preaching.

And, I understand this approach, because "God told me to do this" can be easily and often abused.

But A.W. Tozer disagreed with this approach that disallowed the Spirit's voice.

"I believe that much of our religious unbelief is due to a wrong conception of and a wrong feeling for the Scripture of Truth. A silent God suddenly began to speak in a book and when the book was finished lapsed back into silence again forever? ... with notions like that in our heads how can we believe? ... the Bible will never be a living Book to us until we are convinced that God is articulate in His universe."

Others hear voices everywhere. "God told me to divorce my wife," a wild-eyed man once told me, with absolutely no Biblical grounds for his statement. He was totally convinced that God had spoken to him directly and clearly. "You may have heard a voice," I quietly replied, "but it wasn't God, for he never violates His written Word. He is, of all things, consistent."

God is blamed for a lot. He seems to be telling a lot of people a lot of things that make little sense and glorify everyone but Him. We need balance.

GOD IS SPEAKING THROUGH HIS WORD

"Today if you would *hear* His voice, do not harden your hearts," the Psalmist said. The Word is alive, made so by the presence of the One who is constantly longing to commune with His creation. If you approach the Bible as a dead book you may study its content but you will never know its Author.

> *"I read Thy Word, O, Lord, each passing day and*
> *in Thy sacred page find glad employ, But this I*
> *pray; save from the killing letter.*
> *Teach my heart, set free from human forms the*
> *holy art of reading Thee in every line,*
> *In precept, prophecy, and sign;*
> *Till all my vision filled with Thee, Thy likeness*
> *shall reflect in me;*
> *Not knowledge, but Thyself my joy, for this I pray."*

(*J.C. MacCauley*)

GOD IS SPEAKING BY HIS SPIRIT

> *"For who among men knows the thoughts of a man except*
> *the spirit of the man which is in him? Even so the thoughts*
> *of God no one knows except the Spirit of God. Now we have*
> *received, not the spirit of the world, but the Spirit who is*
> *from God, so that we may know the things freely given to us*
> *by God" (1 Corinthians 2:11-12).*

How can we ignore the quiet, but certain inner witness of the Holy Spirit that has comforted, encouraged, rebuked, corrected and guided God's children for centuries? Our sinfulness and subjectivity make it possible to misread this speaking Voice, but it is speaking nonetheless.

To muzzle God simply because we have abused this is amazingly arrogant. Why would we deny God's ability to continue to speak by His Spirit today? What would cause us to think can we limit God like this?

GOD IS SPEAKING THROUGH HIS PEOPLE

Why would the Bible remind us that "in the abundance of counselors there is victory" if there was not the ability to hear God as He speaks by His Spirit through others? Again, man's sinfulness makes every person's counsel open to evaluation, but is God not powerful enough to speak through another? Not infallibly, but helpfully?

If not, what is the value of preaching? If I did not have the confidence that God could speak as I stood to preach the Word I would think my work is of little value. He spoke through a donkey once; there's hope for me.

GOD IS SPEAKING THROUGH HIS CREATION

"The heavens are telling of the glory of God; and their expanse is declaring the work of His hands. Day to day pours forth speech, and night to night reveals knowledge. There is

no speech, nor are there words; their voice is not heard. Their
line has gone out through all the earth and their utterances
to the end of the world" (Psalm 19:1-4)

If you have not heard God's voice through a thunderstorm
or the singing of a bird you are missing His greatest sym-
phony. I am not speaking of transcendental meditation, but
that the whole earth was created to communicate. To deny
this is to deny its purpose. Those who fail to listen to God's
voice through creation have a one-sided God.

"God is speaking. Not God *spoke*, but God *is speaking*. He
is by His nature continuously articulate. He fills the world
with His speaking Voice," Tozer said. The work of the devot-
ed follower of Christ is to learn to listen, to tune our hearts
to hear. But how?

SITTING DOWN

We must get in the right posture like Mary of Bethany who
was, "seated at the Lord's feet listening to His words." We
must quiet our hearts and "be still and know that He is God."
We must believe in this process knowing "that He is and He
is a rewarder of those who diligently seek Him." We must
be persistent and "ask and keep on asking, seek and keep
on seeking." We must practice till our hearts are attuned to
properly hear, knowing that, "Blessed is the man who listens
to me, watching daily at my gates, waiting at my doorposts"
(Proverbs 8:34).

And when we misread His voice, (which we most surely will do), we must blame ourselves and understand our depravity, not concoct a quick theology that aborts His voice in our lives and the lives of others. Being able to distinguish our mother's voice over a crowd comes from years of hearing. The ability to discern God's true voice from the voice of the world, the flesh, or the devil comes from a long obedience in listening. And we will "know of the teaching that it is Him" as we see fruit from our following.

"The order and life of the world depends upon that Voice, but men are mostly too busy or too stubborn to give attention," Tozer proclaimed. If you deny God access to your life, you are on your own and the world will feel the tragic effect of this loss.

FALLING, BUT NOT FAILING

*"Simon, Simon, behold, Satan demanded to have
you, that he might sift you like wheat, but I have
prayed for you that your faith may not fail. And when
you have turned again, strengthen your brothers."
Peter said to him, "Lord, I am ready to go with you
both to prison and to death.
"Jesus said, "I tell you, Peter, the rooster will not
crow this day, until you deny three times that you
know me."*

(LUKE 22:31-34 ESV)

EVERYBODY DEALS WITH failure. Most men feel like a failure almost all the time in most of the things they do. If we're humble and honest we know that we don't measure up to all we could be. And it haunts us, particularly in times of deep trouble and stress.

WHEN IS FAILURE REAL FAILURE?

Years ago, in a dark, dark time in my extended family, I was deeply struggling with trusting God. It seemed like my world had collapsed. Everything I had held so confidently before was suddenly in question. I had doubts and questions that I had never had before.

The worst part of this whole experience was that I felt I was failing God. I could not seem to "work up" faith and joy in the moment.

One day I came upon this passage above and the precious Spirit began to minister to my heart. I realized Jesus prayed that Peter's faith would not fail. Jesus always prayed perfectly and, therefore, His prayer must have been accomplished. Peter's faith must not have failed, even though he denied Christ.

What was this passage saying? I believe Jesus was saying, (my paraphrase),

> *"Peter, you are about to go through a time when all you have hoped and dreamed for and given your life to is nailed to a cross. It is going to devastate you. It will be a 'sifting' by the enemy of your beliefs so much that you will even come to deny me for a moment.*

> *"But, Peter, I understand this. I know what you're going through and I'm going to do something for you: I AM GOING TO INTERCEDE FOR YOU that your faith would NOT fail. I know my prayer will be answered so, in advance I want to give you instructions in what to do after this grueling experience is over: when you've come through on the other side, strengthen your brothers!"*

A few days later we see Peter sifted by the toughest experience of his life. But we also see him, before the weekend is out, running to the empty tomb. His faith was scratching and clawing and "hoping against hope," but he was there believing. His faith was rewarded and it grew.

The next scene of Peter's life we watch him filled with the Holy Spirit and fire and, as he preaches, 3,000 people are saved!

SURVIVING SATAN'S SIFTER

Sifting is hard. It may take us down to the "slough of despond" in our lives for a season. But there will come a moment of grace when the wind of God's Spirit blows gently across the meager sparks of our faith and it ignites and blazes again.

But sifting is beneficial. It helps us understand others' doubts and fears and struggles. It develops a mature, seasoned faith. It humbles us. It reminds us of God's incredible, personal care of us. It ultimately endears us to Him. It prepares us to be warriors who can face and deal with anything. It toughens us spiritually.

One of my best friends came home one day to find his 14-year-old son murdered in his home. There could be no worse disaster. He was devastated. The next season he was very naturally scrambling, struggling in his faith. But I will never forget what he said to me, in time. "Bill, I have been all the way to the bottom, and it's rock solid!" He has stood for years after this tragic experience and proclaimed the goodness of God even in the midst of a sin-wrecked world, and his life has strengthened and helped thousands.

If you're in the midst of Satan's sifting, be encouraged and don't misinterpret God's agenda. Your Elder Brother is at the right hand of the Father. He is praying for you and your faith will not fail. And, afterward, you will strengthen many!

DAY 32

———— ⬥ ————

GOD'S GLORIOUS LIMITATIONS

The Lord said to Gideon,
"The people who are with you are too many for Me
to give Midian into their hands,
for Israel would become boastful saying 'My own
power has delivered me.'"

(*JUDGES 8:3*)

EVERY CHRISTIAN HAS lived with the seeming lack of God's supply and delay of His timing. We should be filled with gratitude for what He provides, for we deserve nothing. But there are moments when the task is beyond us, the enemies are real, our abilities are insufficient, and the workers are few even after we've prayed for these very things.

And, it's confusing.

CLARIFYING THE MISSION

Our frustration comes from misunderstanding His purpose. God is out to be glorified. Since many of us in our pride will not give Him this honor naturally, He orchestrates experiences where He can remind us of who He is. "God often puts us in situations that are too much for us so we will learn that no situation is too much for him," said Erwin Lutzer. These are the environments where God is magnificently seen.

Bound by this purpose, He is completely capable of resolving everything and always doing that which is "good, acceptable, and perfect" for His children. But it doesn't mean there won't be moments of doubt when we realize we don't have what it takes.

THE REFINING OF FAITH

These are the experiences of faith where God is testing our spiritual constitution. Gideon found his army whittled down from 32,000 to 300 men, all by God's initiation. God was building a faith platform with his humble warrior to show the world His sufficiency.

God has such dexterity that He can accomplish multiple purposes with one stroke. It is nothing for Him to accomplish the task, glorify Himself, train us in faith, and amaze a crowd all at the same time.

I once knew a great Christian leader who lived for these challenges. He was no happier than when confronted with an impossible task that called for a display of God's power. Like Gideon, he saw God manifest Himself in ways many of us envy.

When you find yourself with overwhelming limitations, look for God. He may be orchestrating the whole scenario. He is there and has a bigger agenda than you realize.

DAY 33

ARE YOU THE SURPRISING
LEADER IN THE STORM?

THE BIBLE RECORDS the amazing report of 276 people in the midst of a horrific sea storm. It was so bad that the crew had given up all hope of being saved and had jettisoned the cargo (Acts 27).

But there was one man on the boat that saw things differently. He was a prisoner, of all things, named Paul. But the uniqueness about this man was that he was connected to the God-Who-Oversees-Storms and the One who controls the lives and fortunes of men.

THE WORD

An angel of the Lord appeared to Paul and told him that God had a mission for him to stand before Caesar and give a witness. And, that not one person would perish in the midst of the devastating storm, but that they would all come safely to land. God was determined to save many for the sake of one who would take His message to many.

The storm was so intense, that no logical man who looked at the physical evidence would believe this. It made no human sense, which is the kind of scenario the Divine lovingly orchestrates to display His glory.

THE LEADERSHIP

Suddenly, the prisoner became the leader. "Keep up your courage, men, for I believe God that it will turn out exactly as I have been told," he said (Acts 27:25).

And then he proceeded to eat a meal and told them to join him. "Not a hair from the head of any of your heads will perish," he prophesied, and calmly began to give thanks in the presence of them all and started to eat. It was the worst possible, life-threatening moment, and yet this man is acting like it's a picnic in the park.

All of them were encouraged and began to eat also. This prisoner, announcing an absolutely bizarre possibility in great confidence, became the leader. Why?

FAITH

Faith gives you courage. It grants you the authority to pronounce things that others see as foolish and to do it with such boldness that it ignites faith in them. It makes you the leader, regardless of your human title.

It is important to note, though, that Paul's faith was not presumptuous. It was entirely based on a word given to him by God. And its ultimate purpose was not to exalt Paul, but to exalt God.

ARE YOU LEADING?

In the midst of the incredible swirl around us that is tossing waves and bending the mast of our ship, are you hearing from God as to the true situation? Are you the one who is standing up and announcing God's intentions to a faithless world? Are you bringing to the people around you that which will lift them to faith and bring them safely home? Are you taking your meal calmly and illustrating the bigness of your God?

If not, why not? There could be only two or three reasons. Perhaps you are swayed by the wind yourself and captured in the vortex of humanistic fear. Or, you are not in a position to hear the word of God. Or, you simply will not choose to believe what God is saying.

But, if you want to lead others to Him (and that should be our only real goal in life) you must lead in faith. When you do hear God and stand in faith and lead others to see the God-Who-is-Above-All, then your story will record statements like this at the end of each chapter:

> *"And so it happened that they all were brought
> safely to land."*
>
> *(ACTS 27:44)*

DAY 34

⟨⟩

GOOD POSTURE

O our God, will you not execute judgment on them?
For we are powerless against this great horde that is
coming against us.
We do not know what to do, but our eyes are on you."

(2 CHRONICLES 20:12)

I RECENTLY WENT through a round of physical therapy for my back. To my amazement, the remedy was all about my posture. I was not putting myself in a position to be healed. The way I was standing and sitting was merely compounding the problem.

OUR POSTURE WITH GOD

Many people are never in a position to receive God's blessing. God can do anything He desires at any moment of His choosing. So many of His gifts are given when we least deserve it. His "rain" falls on the just and the unjust and in His "kindness He leads us to repentance."

But there are certain things God has committed Himself to do in this age only as we place ourselves in the way of blessing. "I will do this, if you will do this," He often promises. God longs for us to come to Him and trust Him. Each exercise is designed to bring us to the place of greater faith.

Jehoshaphat got in the right posture, at least in one season of his life. When faced with an overwhelming enemy he didn't try to manipulate or give a show of his human strength.

HIS PLEA
"O our God, will you not execute judgment on them?" (Vs. 12)

He reminds God of His peculiar relationship with His children. He is their Father and on the basis of God's honor, Jehoshaphat cries to God to deliver proper judgment to his enemies.

HIS CONFESSION
"For we are powerless" (Vs. 12)

It takes most of us a long time to get here. Some, sadly, never do. Blindly convinced of their ability to handle anything, they plunge ahead in life and never experience God.

HIS FAITH
"We do not know what to do, but our eyes are on You." (Vs. 12)

This good leader's greatest passion was not mere physical deliverance, but God. God would show them. God would deliver them. God was what they needed—not a program or a new plan, but a Person. He knew that anything *more* than God was not needed; anything *less* than God was inadequate.

The particular situations you find yourself in, perhaps even right now, are all a part of a Divine design to bring you before Him with a plea, a confession, and a trusting focus. God wants you *before* Him. Humbly looking up to Him should be your unceasing posture. And He crowns these moments with the blessings that can only be provided from His all-sufficient hand.

DAY 35

GOD'S FAITH

"For we are God's fellow workers; you are God's field"

(I CORINTHIANS 3:9)

HE MUST THINK a lot of us. That God would make us major players in redeeming the world is mind-boggling. We think so lightly of ourselves, but apparently God does not. He believes in what He created.

GOD BELIEVES IN HIS PEOPLE
God's confidence springs out of the various components of His people and plan. He knows He has saved multiple people with varying personalities and spiritual gifts to accomplish the task. This community called the church is ultimately effective. Glance at history. We may not understand the process, but God knows what He's about.

We look at the sin in the church (which is very apparent); God sees people who are fearfully and wonderfully made. We see our unfaithfulness; He observes the spiritual gifts He has sovereignly placed among us. We look at our weakness; He sees the sufficiency of His grace to empower us. We look at the lateness of the hour; He rests in His timing to sovereignly bring others to Himself. We see the desperate need for revival in our nation, (and we should), but we should not be faithlessly despairing. Around the world, tens of thousands of people are being saved every day! We are horrified at how poorly we're doing; He believes that the "gates of hell will not prevail" against His church.

GOD BELIEVES IN HIS PLAN

Can you imagine that God would leave this to chance or our sinful unfaithfulness? Like a wise farmer who allows his children to work in His fields, He will not let the field be unproductive. He oversees this project with meticulous precision. He may use others if we fail in faithfulness, but He will not allow His harvest to spoil in the field.

And He trusts Himself. "I planted," said Paul, "Apollos watered, but God caused the growth." God is the initiator, opening blinded eyes, drawing sinners, giving grace, saving lives. He's not only good at His task, He's perfect.

Paul knew this. It spurred him to restful, but aggressive labor. "I am confident that He who began a good work in you will bring it to completion" (Philippians 1:6). This God-confidence should not cause us to relax our hands, but move us with gratitude to the greater work. We are co-workers with God! What a privilege and opportunity. Rise up and meet the day!

DAY 36

THE STRUGGLE THAT DESTROYS
AND REMAKES US

*"I have seen God face to face and yet my life has
been delivered."*

(GENESIS 32:30)

IT IS DOUBTFUL that any man will be changed into Christ's likeness without moments of intense battle. The flesh dies hard.
God, in His infinite jealousy for His chosen children, often
boxes us in by simply letting us have our own way.

He knows that, given enough rope, we will hang ourselves and that only when the noose is around our neck will
we be ready to turn to Him in brokenness, repentance and
faith. As Tozer said, "It is doubtful if God can use a man
greatly unless He hurts him deeply."

THE JACOB SYNDROME

We are most like Jacob. He was an independent, sinful, devi-
ous man. All of his life he had known something of God, but
not enough. He had known God through his heritage, but
not his experience. In His mercy, God had protected Jacob

119

enough so that he would not destroy himself, but let him loose enough to bring him to a Jabbok moment.

One lonely night Jacob found himself with his angry father-in-law behind him and his estranged brother, Esau in front of him. He was hemmed in by the consequences of his own ways. This is where his self-life had placed him and it was a frightful spot, alone by the Jabbok river. In the darkness of the night, Jacob felt the crushing weight of his own choices, as God was deliberately bringing him to the end of himself.

THE JABBOK ENCOUNTER

At that precise moment he encountered God and it was not pleasant. We will only discover the nature of this night in eternity, but it is described as "wrestling." All night long, Jacob and the Lord fought with each other. As the morning dawns, Jacob's Divine opponent had "not prevailed against him" and so "He touched the socket of his thigh; so the socket of Jacob's thigh was dislocated while he wrestled with him" (Genesis 32:25). God gave the needed disabling blow.

Finally the limping wrestler realized that God and God alone was the Source. No one else could save Him. None but God could bless Him, and He cried out for God.

This is the point of the exercise. Now God is free to give the blessing He was after all along: He changed Jacob. This transformation was accompanied by the bestowing of a new name. The sinful Jacob became the devout Israel and was now ready to walk into the fullness of his destiny.

THE PENIEL ALTAR

Now, like his father and grandfather before Him, the knowing Israel could build an altar of true worship. He was no longer a spectator but a willing participant in God's redemptive history.

> *The great preacher Martyn Lloyd-Jones was once asked, "What does a person look like who has truly met God?" Alluding to Genesis 32:31, he replied, "He walks with a limp." After encountering the living Christ, Jacob was forever crippled—both physically and in regard to his ego. He could no longer strut around arrogantly as he had done before. His pride turned to lowliness (33:3). His greed turned to generosity (33:10–11). And his self-reliance had turned into worship (33:20). So we who are professing believers must ask ourselves: Have these things happened to me? Have my habits changed? Have I met the Lord? (Strassner, Opening Up Genesis)*

If you have not come to the Jabbok you may still vainly believe that your plans will work, your strength is sufficient, and your wisdom is impeccable. A life of self-trust. If you sense that may be so, cry out for the Jabbok. Ask God to take you there.

It may be that only a lonely night at the Jabbok and a sweaty striving with your Master will work this out of you and bring you to humble faith. It may be a long night, but it will hurt you in the best possible way.

DAY 37

THE FIVE MARKS OF TRULY GREAT LEADERS

LEADERSHIP IS HARD. But, for those who are connected to God, it doesn't have to be complicated. With God in the equation, clear direction and effectiveness can be discovered.

A young shepherd boy who had learned to trust God in the hills of Judea is one of our greatest examples of faith-filled leadership. His life overflows with great leadership characteristics.

HUMILITY

David was one of the greatest leaders in human history. But his leadership legacy begins and ends with his humility.

> *And David knew that the Lord had established him as king over Israel, and that his kingdom was highly exalted for the sake of his people Israel. (1 Chronicles 14:2)*

David knew who had made him king and why. He did not suffer under the delusion that it was his ability or power that placed him in this position of responsibility. He also understood that the purpose of his position was not about him. He was a leader for the sake of God's people.

Pride always aborts great leadership. A massive study was done by a secular organization that produced the book "Good to Great" by Jim Collins (a tremendously helpful read). Over many years they tried to identify the five characteristics that made good companies great. They wanted to avoid the obvious issue of leadership, but in the end, they could not. In every case they found the single, greatest component was a leader whose strongest characteristics were humility and ser-vanthood. A strong, but unassuming leader who passionately served for the sake of the mission.

If you want to be a great leader, this issue must be settled. It is not about you. God exalts one and puts down another and He has a plan. Your current position is not a stair step in your resume, but an opportunity to accomplish God's agenda for the lives of people. A leader is a servant placed in his position by God and must stay wrapped in the servant's apron of humility. It is the noble robe of every great leader.

DEPENDENCY AND OBEDIENCE

A truly humble leader knows his source. Compelled by that understanding, he continually turns to God for direction. With that direction, he humbly and quickly obeys.

And David inquired of God, "Shall I go up against the Philistines? Will you give them into my hand?" And the Lord said to him, "Go up, and I will give them into your hand." And he went up to Baal-Perazim, and David struck them down there. And David said, "God has broken through my enemies by my hand, like a bursting flood." (1 Chronicles 14:10-11)

PERSEVERANCE

There are many one-shot wonders in the leadership ranks. Leaders who secured one victory and then faded. A mark of great leaders is perseverance. They are wise enough to keep depending upon the Lord with each new decision.

Some leaders experience a victory by God and they program the pattern, assuming that the Lord will always work the same way. Or, perhaps they forget that it was the Lord who directed them and they think they can win the next battle on their own (which was King Saul's fatal flaw). David, however, kept inquiring. In the next battle, God had a different plan. But David humbly listened, genuinely trusted, and fully obeyed.

And the Philistines yet again made a raid in the valley. And when David again inquired of God, God said to him, "You shall not go up after them; go around and come against them opposite the balsam trees. And when you hear the sound of marching in the tops of the balsam trees, then go out to battle, for God has gone out before you to strike down the army of the Philistines." And David did as God commanded him, and they struck down the Philistine army from Gibeon to Gezer. (1 Chronicles 14:13-16)

GRATITUDE

The final exam of leadership, though, is the hardest. When results occur, natural accolades follow. This is the acid test of humble leadership. The best leaders are filled with gratitude. They keep deferring all praise to the real Leader in the equation. They remember the source. They know that any fame has come from God's activity through them and those who serve with them. They are simply God's servants. They will be exalted in due time by Him, and that is enough.

> *And David said, "God has broken through my enemies by my hand, like a bursting flood" (1 Chronicles 14:10-11).*

> *And the fame of David went out into all lands, and the Lord brought the fear of him upon all nations (1 Chronicles 14:17).*

Leadership is hard and those who navigate well to the finish line are rare. But for anyone who desires to be a truly great leader there is an amazing simplicity. Remember who put you in leadership and why. Humbly, dependently listen to the Lord and do exactly what He says, letting Him literally lead through you. Maintain this pattern consistently and give Him *all* the glory.

--- ❦ ---

REALISTIC FAITH

REMEMBER THE STORY of the twin boys with opposite personalities? One was a miserable pessimist, the other an incurable optimist. The parents, seeking to balance the two, gave the pessimist a new bike for Christmas and the optimist a bag of horse manure.

Christmas morning came. The parents asked the pessimist, "Do you like your new bike?" He replied, "It's okay, but it will probably rust and I'll have a wreck and cut myself and probably have to go to the hospital."

Realizing their experiment had failed, they asked, "Where's your brother?" To which he replied, "Oh, he got all excited and went outside saying something about trying to find his new horse!"

Everybody looks at life from the up or down side. Part of this is personality, (one of the reasons we need the balance of each person). But another part is faith as we see in the Apostle Paul.

As he describes his ministry in 2 Corinthians 4:8-18, we could take just one side of the equation, which is what some people do to their great detriment.

I am ...

1. *Afflicted*
2. *Perplexed*
3. *Persecuted*

4. *Struck down*
5. *Always dying*
6. *Death is working in me*
7. *My outer man is decaying*

If this is your only witness to a watching world, it is a poor representation of the power of Christ. Unbelievers would rightly say, "Why would I want to be a follower of Christ and add extra weight to my backpack? I've got enough problems already!"

Others view their lives and ministries from an eternal, heavenly perspective and say this about their situation.

I am ...

1. *Not crushed!*
2. *Not despairing!*
3. *Not forsaken!*
4. *Not destroyed!*
5. *Life is manifested in my body!*
6. *Life is coming to others!*
7. *My inner man is being renewed day by day!*

But, if this is the only testimony you give, some may think you are in denial about life's realities or that you have never encountered the difficulties they are facing.

STRIKING THE BALANCE
The best possible way to view life as a child of God is to join the two, just as Paul did. This admits the reality of your

current condition, but confesses the greater reality of God's abundant grace to overwhelmingly conquer through Jesus Christ our Lord!

I am ...

1.   *Afflicted, but not crushed!*
2.   *Perplexed, but not despairing!*
3.   *Persecuted, but not forsaken!*
4.   *Struck down, but not destroyed!*
5.   *Always carrying about in the body the dying of Jesus, so that the life of Jesus also may be manifested in our body!*
6.   *So death works in us, but life in you!*
7.   *Though my outer man is decaying, my inner man is being renewed day by day!*

LOOK UP!

So how do you get there? How do you maintain a witness of great victory in the midst of the pain of this world and the press of ministry? The key is an eternal perspective and simple faith in the God who IS!

*"For momentary, light affliction is producing for us an eternal weight of glory far beyond all comparison, while we **look** not at the things which are seen, but at the things which are not seen; for the things which are seen are temporal, but the*

things which are not seen are eternal" (2 Corinthians 4:17-18, emphasis mine).

If your vision is not aerated by heaven's reality you will be overwhelmed and discouraged. The authentic man of faith is a realist in both directions. He recognizes life's problems, but also the solutions. The pain, but the power. The overwhelming odds, but the overarching grace.

The world needs to see a robust faith. A faith that is overcoming in the midst of difficulty. This gives authenticity and hope to everyone who observes us, no matter the current situation, and points them to our sufficient God.

DAY 39

—— ❦ ——

ENTERING IN

Most people live on the east side of the Jordan. Like the Israelite fathers, they have come to the Promised Land but stepped back because they see life with only their physical eyes. They do not agree in faith with God's promise that their giants will "be like bread" to them. And they wander and die in the wilderness because of their unbelief.

But there are those blessed ones who enter into the promises of God though faith. They conquer. They enjoy the best God has designed. Joshua and his followers are designed to be a model for us in this regard. A picture of faith that enters in.

THE EXPECTANCY OF FAITH

Then Joshua rose early in the morning; and he and all the sons of Israel set out from Shittim and came to the Jordan. (Joshua 3:1)

Suddenly one morning, Joshua and his people find themselves standing right on the edge of the raging, Jordan river. For forty years they had not been here. What changed? God had spoken His word to a humble leader's heart, it birthed faith, and Joshua stood up to lead with spiritual conviction. The people headed out, expecting God to take them into Canaan.

Matthew Henry said, "We must go on in the way of our duty though we foresee difficulties, trusting God to help us through them when we come to them. Let us proceed as far as we can, and depend on Divine sufficiency for that which we find ourselves insufficient." The expectancy of faith brought them to the Jordan for the first time in 40 years. True faith leads us in anticipation right to the edge of the promises.

THE OBEDIENCE OF FAITH

At the end of three days the officers went through the midst of the camp; and they commanded the people, saying, "When you see the ark of the covenant of the Lord your God with the Levitical priests carrying it, then you shall set out from your place and go after it." (Vs. 2-4)

Their expectations would have been meaningless had they not followed in obedient faith. They were instructed to "Go after it!" And what were they to follow? The presence of God.

This is the essence of faith: simply following Christ! Pursuing Him. Getting into the position to see where He is going and joining Him. It is not to pursue a program or a personality. Faith sees Christ as its object and daily, hourly draws near to Him.

THE CONSECRATION OF FAITH

Then Joshua said to the people, "Consecrate yourselves, for tomorrow the Lord will do wonders among you." (Vs. 5)

Joshua knew that to go where Christ was leading would require a fresh level of spiritual intentionality. They could not follow Him carelessly. They were to cleanse and prepare themselves. To remove any impediment that would weigh them down.

The writer of Hebrews would reiterate this consecration to us, thousands of years later. We are to "lay aside every encumbrance and the sin which so entangles us and let us run with endurance the race that is set before us, fixing our eyes on Jesus" (Hebrews 12:1).

No one will cross the Jordan, bring down the walls of Jericho, and conquer the giants in life if they are unwilling to pursue "the sanctification without which no one will see the Lord" (Hebrews 12:14).

THE WONDERS OF FAITH!

" for tomorrow the Lord will do wonders among you." (Vs. 5)

God intentionally led Joshua and the people to the Jordan during the harvest season, when the river was raging and overflowing its banks. But the instant the priests put their feet in the water, (a true step of faith), the waters stood up in one heap and parted from the city of Adam to the Dead Sea—a distance of 30 miles! The Divine breath dried the riverbed and the raging obstacle became a super-highway into God's promises.

God has not changed and His principles of faith are identical to what Joshua utilized. We may explain that our inactivity is simply waiting on God to part the waters. But God is waiting on our expectant, obedient, consecrated faith to follow Him into the Jordan and across to His promises!

DAY 40

───── ❦ ─────

THE LAST 10% OF FAITH

*"Trust in the Lord with all your heart and do not
lean on your own understanding.
In all your ways acknowledge Him and He will
direct your paths."*

(PROVERBS 3:5-6)

I HEARD A great Christian leader say that the toughest part of
many conversations with others is always the last 10%. You've
covered a lot of ground in the first 90% of the conversation,
but there is something that you really need to discuss with
them. It may even be the reason you initiated the conversation. Getting to that last (and usually most vital) part of the
discussion takes some risk and a lot of courage. Good leaders
have learned to push through to the final words.

GOD'S AGENDA

The maturing believer understands that God's whole agenda
with us is to restore us to a position of trust in Him. It's always about faith. When you read the great roll call of leaders
in Hebrews, Chapter 11, it is not a description of random

qualities. They were great men and women because they were all great in faith and "without faith it is impossible to please God" (Hebrews 11:6).

God is a relentless teacher. He orchestrates circumstances with amazing precision to stretch our belief in Him. Solomon saw this under the inspiration of the Spirit and encouraged us to "trust in the Lord" (the positive command), and "do not lean on your own understanding" (the negative command).

It seems these are the only two options in any decision. To choose the latter is to rest upon your meager abilities, touched by the fall. A pathetic but most common response. To trust in the Lord is to bring God and all the resources of heaven into the equation. This honors Him by illustrating we believe in His goodness and greatness enough to follow Him fully.

THE PARAMETERS OF FAITH

So Solomon urges us to full faith in two exacting ways: *all our heart—all our ways.* We are masters of creating pockets of unbelief. Little closets where we hide an issue from God. And God wants it all.

Most believers find it easy to trust God about some things, but "all our ways?"

- *"My finances? Lord, I got myself in to this mess, surely you must want me to get myself out through my own thinking and manipulation?"*

- *"My reputation? Lord, you don't know how they are. If I don't make sure they know what I've done and stick up for my rights I'll never get to the position I need or revenge I desire."*
- *"My relationships? God, these need a little help from me. I cannot just do what's right and trust you with the results."*

Faith must also invade "all our heart." We constantly wrestle doubt and fear. He longs for us to mature to full faith from head to toe. To come to the point where we see Him as all faithful. Where there is no crevice of our mind or heart where we are not releasing all to His control.

THE REWARD OF FULL FAITH

God binds Himself with a sacred promise that is hard to believe. If we will trust Him with "all our heart," and in "all our ways acknowledge Him," He says that "He will direct our paths." This is what we wanted all along, isn't it? To know God's will and direction? To be led by the One who needs no leadership and is perfect in all His ways? To find that guidance that is found nowhere else?

Where is the last 10% for you? It's time to cross the line of faith.

OTHER WRITINGS BY BILL ELLIFF

OneCry!
A Nationwide Call for Spiritual Awakening
(Byron Paulus and Bill Elliff)

The Presence-Centered Church

Whitewater
Navigating the Rapids of Church Conflict

Forgiveness
Healing the Harbored Hurts of your Heart

Lifting the Load
How to Gain and Maintain a Clear Conscience

Everyman . . . *the Rescue*

50 Marks of a Man of God
Important Questions for those in Spiritual Leadership

Personal Revival Checklist
A Spiritual Evaluation through the Sermon on the Mount

Turning the Tide
Having MORE Kids who Follow Christ
(Holly Elliff with Bill Elliff)

Order at www.billelliff.org (bulk prices on request)

Made in the USA
San Bernardino, CA
16 August 2016